The Four Cornerstones

CLAUDE "BUTCH" HARMON, JR.
AND JOHN ANDRISANI

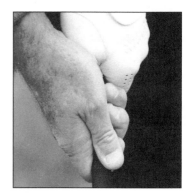

# of Winning Golf

A FIRESIDE BOOK
Published by Simon & Schuster

FIRESIDE
Rockefeller Center
1230 Avenue of the Americas
New York, NY 10020

First Fireside Edition 1997

FIRESIDE and colophon are registered trademarks
of Simon & Schuster Inc.

DESIGNED BY BARBARA MARKS
Manufactured in the United States of America

10 9 8 7 6 5 4 3 2 1

The Library of Congress has cataloged the Simon & Schuster edition as follows:

Harmon, Claude, date.
The four cornerstones of winning golf / Claude "Butch" Harmon,
Jr., and John Andrisani.
p.   cm.
Includes index.
1. Golf.   I. Andrisani, John.   II. Title.
GV965.H274   1996
796.352—dc20   96-7316   CIP

ISBN 0-684-80792-0
ISBN 0-684-83404-9 (Pbk)

To my wife, Lillie, my daughter, Michaele Anne, and my son, Claude:
for their love and support, and the sacrifices they made
that allowed me to pursue my dream of becoming a respected teacher,
to both amateur players and top Tour professionals.

Contents

The Four Cornerstones of Winning Golf

Introduction

I owe my life to my dad, Claude Harmon, Sr., a golf professional who surprised the world with a win in the 1948 Masters, one of the game's four major championships. My father was a club pro, and club pros are not supposed to win high-caliber tournaments. Only seasoned Tour pros are supposed to do that, so the sports press had a field day in the spring of 1948 when my dad took home the coveted green jacket.

At the time of his victory I was not quite 5 years old. Yet, even at that early age, I thought there was nobody greater at golf than my dad, so I wasn't surprised by his win.

After starting to play golf at age 6, I appreciated the magnitude of my dad's accomplishment. However, in the years that followed, I respected him more for his teaching skills than his playing abilities.

No teacher could spot and correct a swing fault faster than my father. No instructor could teach a rank beginner to play golf as fast as my dad. My father had a great eye. He was also a great motivator and communicator. Like all quality teachers, he was patient and kept things simple, and he had a wonderful sense of humor, which helped him and the student get by on those rare bad days.

I can't say that I learned everything there is to know about golf from my dad. But I sure can say that I learned almost everything. My father inspired me to learn about the golf swing, and the art of shotmaking and scoring—so much so that, at age 8, I gave my first lesson to my brother Craig. And what I didn't learn from Dad, I learned from his golfing buddies, including the great Ben Hogan.

Speaking of Mr. Hogan, my dad told him all about a book he was writing on golf instruction. In fact, a foreword written by Mr. Hogan was supposed to be included in that very book. My father never finished that book. Unfortunately, he passed away first, leaving me and my three brothers—Craig, Dick, and Billy, all golf pros—to carry on the family teaching tradition.

Many of the swing and shotmaking principles that would have been included in my dad's book are in the one you now hold in your hands. *The Four Cornerstones of Winning Golf* is based largely on notes left behind by my father, conversations I had with him, and observations I made while taking lessons from him or while watching him teach members of Winged Foot and Seminole Golf Clubs. The same basic swing keys that I taught to Greg Norman, Davis Love III, and Tiger Woods were passed on to me by my dad, as were all but a few of the other tips contained in this

Me, at age 8, giving a lesson to my brother Craig.

book on the setup, the swing, ball striking, the short game, and curing common faults.

Under the circumstances, I think it only fitting that I include in this book the foreword that Mr. Hogan wrote for my dad. It reads as follows:

The writer of this book is a learner, teacher, player, and an excellent club professional. He is blessed with a very pleasant personality and his enthusiasm for golf is unlimited.

Many years ago when I first met Claude Harmon, a slender kid, and was with him on occasion, I came to realize he would become a master professional. He has gone beyond my expectations.

Because of his inquisitive attitude toward the golf swing, and using a process of elimination and simplification, he arrived at a point where he could literally put a golf swing together piece by piece—just as a watchmaker would while making a watch. Not only did he put these parts together for himself by winning the Masters Tournament, but also for others.

He has an unselfish yen to help others mold a golf game together, not only from a swing standpoint but from a scoring standpoint as well. Proof of this is quite evident when thinking back to what some of his former assistants have accomplished. To name a few—Jack Burke, Mike Souchak, Dave Marr, and Shelly Mayfield, all major winners on the tour.

For years Claude has held two club professional positions in the same year, one in the summer and one in the winter, both masterfully operated.

The readers of this book will subtract [sic] a wealth of enjoyable information fom a fine man who is remarkably dedicated to golf.

BEN HOGAN

When Mr. Hogan sent this foreword to my dad, it was accompanied by a cover letter that included these words: *I am looking forward to a copy of your book, for I know it will be pleasant and informative reading.*

I hope when Mr. Hogan reads the copy of *The Four Cornerstones of Winning Golf* that I sent him, he feels I did my father justice.

CLAUDE HARMON, JR.

My Game

and Yours

ON LEARNING GOLF,

PLAYING GOLF, AND

TEACHING PEOPLE HOW TO PLAY GOLF

On April 11, 1948, members of two prestigious golf clubs—Seminole in North Palm Beach, Florida, and Winged Foot in Mamaroneck, New York—clanged glasses of champagne, guzzled beer, sipped Scotch whisky, and sang "For He's a Jolly Good Fellow" at their respective 19th holes into the wee hours of the morning, to celebrate the great achievement of one of their own. Claude Harmon, the same pro who taught them on Sunday mornings how to cure a vicious slice or splash the ball out of sand, had just won the highly coveted Masters championship.

I was 4 years old at the time of my father's victory. I was staying in Augusta, Georgia, where the Masters is played every year, with my mom and dad. Dad came in late after a night of celebration. According to my mom, when he returned, he covered me with the green jacket they give to the Masters winner, a gesture that made perfect sense since Dad always shared everything with his family.

Played over the hilly and highly demanding Augusta National Golf Club course, the Masters, along with the U.S. Open, the PGA, and the British Open, is one of golf's four major championships. For a big-name pro to win this prestigious event was one thing. That was expected. What wasn't expected was a little-known self-taught pro shooting a record-tying score of 279, over 72 holes, to beat his nearest rival, Cary Middlecoff, by five strokes, and such seasoned stars as Ben Hogan, Byron Nelson, Sam Snead, and Gene Sarazen, by even bigger margins. According to star gazers and golf aficionados, this wasn't supposed to happen. After all, club pros watch the bad swings of members all day long, have little time to practice, and are not accustomed to playing under pressure. Claude Harmon sure proved the press, and all other doubters, wrong.

Over the years I asked my dad, hundreds of times, about that vic-

Even though my dad was an underdog, he showed the quiet confidence of a winner after the third round of the 1948 Masters, when he stood before the scoreboard as the 54-hole leader.

tory—how he clinched it with a birdie, birdie, eagle run on holes 6, 7, and 8 of the final round—and, as always, he was very modest in his explanation. Instead of taking full credit for shooting scores of 70, 70, 69, and 70, he repeatedly thanked Craig Wood, his former boss at Winged Foot, for teaching him a lot about golf swing technique. Ironically, Wood was the head professional at Winged Foot when he, too, won a Masters—his in 1941.

Prior to the 1948 Masters, Wood shared his local knowledge about Augusta National with Dad, and told him which shots he should practice. Consequently, Dad was ready for battle.

According to Dad, another reason he was able to hit such spectacular shots and shoot under par the final day to clinch the Masters was that he worked at Seminole and Winged Foot: two clubs with world-class courses that forced him to become an accurate striker of the ball and an inventive shotmaker. To put it simply, at both courses, but at Winged Foot particularly, you had to hit straight drives to avoid playing an approach shot through trees; you had to be a master of sand and an expert chipper and pitcher too, if you wanted to save par from close by the greens.

There are two courses at Winged Foot Golf Club, the West and the East, both designed in 1923 by Albert W. Tillinghast, an architectural genius with a flair for hazards.

Both courses, situated on rolling terrain, feature tree-lined fairways and undulated greens of sundry shapes and sizes. The East Course has been the venue for two women's United States Open championships. The West Course, the longer and the most famous of this dynamic duo, has hosted four United States Open Golf Championships: in 1929, 1959, 1974, and 1984. Both courses are very challenging. The West, however, is the one that demands the greatest degree of controlled length off the tee. It demands cool nerves, too, when hitting approach shots through shoots of tall oak trees to elevated greens surrounded by steep-faced bunkers.

The Seminole Golf Club was started by E. F. Hutton, whose Wall Street cronies, along with the duPonts, Baruchs, Kennedys, Phippses, and other socialite families, popularized this winter wonderland. The fact that His Royal Highness, the Duke of Windsor, cited Seminole as one of his favorite courses made the Palm Beach club an even more special place.

The Seminole golf course was designed by Donald Ross, the renowned course architect whose other most famous works include Pinehurst Number Two in North Carolina, Oakland Hills in Michigan, Inverness and Scioto in Ohio, and Oak Hill in New York.

In building Seminole, Ross was influenced by the layout of Royal Dornoch, a spectacular course located in Dornoch, Scotland, his hometown.

One of Ross's trademarks, and a throwback to Dornoch, was the

Jack Burke, Jr., one of my early mentors.

Me and my trusty 7-wood.

crown green at the top of an upslope. There are several of those to test even the nerves of scratch players and visiting pros at Seminole.

Ross had a flair for creating hazards, too, which is why the numerous pure white sand traps, all strategically placed around Seminole's fairly long layout, are no surprise. Should you be fortunate and play Seminole one day, you'll never forget the 16th hole, a dogleg-right par four that features a sea of sand surrounding a green that has the Atlantic Ocean as its backdrop.

Because of my father, I was lucky to be able to play at these great courses with some of the greatest names in golf.

By the time I was 6 years old, I had a club in my hand, a shortened 7-wood that my father gave me. Dad told me to swing this club as hard as I could, because he always believed, as I do now, that it's easier to get a student to slow down his swing later in life than it is to get him to speed it up.

Early on, I was taught the basic fundamentals by my dad and his assistant at Winged Foot, Jack Burke, Jr., another fine player who went on to win the 1956 Masters and PGA championships.

When I was 8, Dad encouraged me to learn to play under pressure. He'd have me challenge the members at Seminole when they played the par-four 6th hole near our on-course home. I would drop a ball down about a hundred yards from the green, then bet the members a package of Life Savers that I could "get home."

Tommy Armour—one of the all-time great teachers—showed me how to hit a variety of shots.

As I grew older, I learned much more about the art of shot-making and scoring. Dad's assistants—Mike Souchak, Dick Mayer, and Dave Marr, who all went on to win major championships—shared swing secrets with me. Tommy Armour, one of the all-time greats from Scotland, and Craig Wood both taught me some things about shotmaking as well. Dad, however, who incidentally held the course records at both Winged Foot courses with a score of 61, remained my chief mentor, particularly when it came to the subject of practice.

Like Ben Hogan, Dad was big on practice. Unlike Hogan, however, he didn't spend most of his hours trying to perfect the golf swing. Most of his time was spent practicing the short game. That was also what he encouraged me to do.

When I asked him why he had me hit so many chips, pitches, and sand shots, he explained that 65 percent of all shots are played from 100 yards in from the green.

My practice sessions with Dad were anything but run of the mill. To prepare me for serious competition, he'd have me hit shag bags of balls from different lies: chips and pitches from manicured fairway grass, light rough, deep rough, hardpan, and divot holes. In addition, he'd have me experiment with different clubs.

Furthermore, with the goal in mind to teach me how to become a creative shotmaker, he'd have me set the clubface square, open, or closed, so I would learn how the ball reacted in the air and on the ground.

When it came time to practice sand shots, I didn't learn how to recover from only good lies. I had to play from buried lies, downhill lies, uphill lies, and sidehill lies. Also, Dad would have me hit shots from bunkers using a 4- or 5-iron. That drill taught me that the proper technique—a right-hand controlled method (where the right hand dominates throughout the entire backswing and downswing)—was more critical to recovering than using a sand wedge, the normal club for playing out of bunkers.

When I finally got the chance to hit drives, Dad had me purposely try to hit fades and draws. I was never allowed to hit more than eight shots in a row in the same direction. That practice strategy kept my concentration powers sharp, and taught me how to work the ball in different wind conditions. Besides that, it got me used to hitting tee shots on holes that curved right or left.

To enhance my creativity and ability to play iron shots, Dad had me practice hitting off different lies, to ever-changing targets. Plus, he had me choke down sometimes to see how that affected distance control. Out on the course, he allowed me to play only even-numbered irons one day, odd-numbered irons the next. This forced me to be more inventive in my shotmaking. For example, if the distance called for a 6-iron, and I had to play an odd-numbered club, I learned how to play an easy 5-iron or a hard 7-iron instead, to reach the green.

Although at the time this stringent and unorthodox form of practice made little sense to me, and sometimes seemed more torturous than enjoyable, it paid off greatly. I soon realized Dad's master plan. I was practicing my weaknesses instead of my strengths, which made me a much more well-rounded shotmaker. Furthermore, this manner of practice readied me for anything the golf gods threw at me in tournament play.

During my teens, when not caddying for Dad and learning more and more about golf technique, I played in junior competitions, including three United States Junior championships.

In those days, my idol was Arnold Palmer, who my dad said I patterned my "physical" swing after. However, I learned more from Ben Hogan, one of the game's all-time best ball strikers and course strategists.

My dad had played many rounds with Hogan, and taught him how to hit a few fancy shots along the way. As a result, Mr. Hogan took great pleasure in educating me on two important aspects of the game: course management and the mental side of golf.

I played with Mr. Hogan in 1960 at the Meadow Brook Club on Long Island, New York. By that time, Mr. Hogan had won two PGA championships, four U.S. Open titles, two Masters, and one British Open; so I truly shook like a leaf on the first tee. Nevertheless, I returned a respectable score of 78. Hogan's score was 75, but his score wasn't what impressed me. It was how he shot that score. What I learned from him that day I have never forgotten, and for that reason I teach these valuable lessons to my students:

Arnold Palmer, one of my golf idols while I was growing up.

- Don't always select a driver to tee off with on a par-four or par-five hole.
- A fade is a much more highly controlled shot than a draw.
- Make a practice swing that is the exact rehearsal of the swing you intend to put on the ball.
- Set up the same way every time to play a particular club, unless you're hitting a specialty shot, such as a draw or low punch.
- Stare at the area of fairway where you want your tee shot to land.
- Take time to visualize the shot you intend to hit.
- Plan ahead on approach shots, so that if you mishit the ball you are left with a relatively easy chip to save par.
- Don't get upset by bad holes.

Hole	Champ Course	Reg. Course	Ladies Course	Par	St'kes	Self	Part'r	Opp.	Opp.	Hole	Champ Course	Reg. Course	Ladies Course	Par	St'kes	Self	Part'r	Opp.	Opp.
	REPLACE TURF SMOOTH FOOT PRINTS IN BUNKERS					*Butch*	*Ben*	*Paul*			MEADOW BROOK CLUB WESTBURY L. I.					*B*	*BEN*	*P S*	
1	360	351	296	4	18	4	4	4	6	10	460	450	377	4	5	4	3	4	4
2	211	190	164	3	16	3	4	3	4	11	426	415	350	4	7	4	5	4	5
3	435	415	350	4	6	5	6	6	5	12	412	404	327	4	3	4	4	4	5
4	480	472	406	5	14	4	6	4	5	13	165	165	125	3	17	3	3	3	4
5	216	208	150	3	12	3	3	3	4	14	434	411	313	4	13	5	5	4	5
6	439	430	375	4	2	5	4	4	5	15	344	336	291	4	15	4	4	4	5
7	427	393	335	4	8	4	6	4	4	16	268	230	194	3	11	3	3	4	4
8	556	548	509	5	10	5	6	6	6	17	428	413	326	4	9	5	4	4	6
9	436	422	362	4	4	4	3	4	5	18	625	590	523	5	1	5	5	6	6
Out	3560	3429	2947	36		37	42	38	45	In	3562	3414	2826	35		37	36	37	
Player										Out	3560	3429	2947	36		74	78	75	
Player										Total	7122	6843	5773	71					
Player										HANDICAP									
Player										NET									
Date																			

My most famous scorecard, from my game with Ben Hogan and friends.

- Don't get overexcited or overconfident because you played a hole particularly well.
- Concentrate only on hitting fairways and greens.
- Stay patient and good scores will come.

Mr. Hogan's lessons, along with those from my dad, plus the swing and shotmaking tips given to me by the many top pros who played "The Foot," helped me improve quickly during my teenage years.

The highlight of these years was my 8 and 7 victory over Mike Turnesa, Jr., in the finals of the Metropolitan Junior, played in 1961 at the Inwood Country Club in New York. My opponent's uncle, Jim Turnesa, had won the 1952 PGA championship, so the local press had a field day building up a rivalry, then reporting it in the newspapers.

My impressive record in junior high and high school golf earned me a scholarship to the University of Houston, a school that over the years has produced a long list of Tour professionals.

Houston seemed to be the perfect place for me to learn a secondary profession and prepare myself competitively for a career on the PGA Tour. To make a short story shorter, it didn't work out. I didn't like the school or the state, something I find particularly amusing now since I live in Texas today.

I played on the PGA Tour as an amateur in 1962 to see if I had the ingredients that were needed for earning a living week after week. That was pressure enough. But, quite frankly, there were other pressures that were surfacing. Being the son of Claude Harmon, I was sort of in a Catch-22 situation. If I won tournaments, people would say, "Well, of course Butch played well, he's Harmon's kid." If I failed, they'd say, "Can't understand it, how come Harmon's son can't get his game up to Tour standard?"

Not sure whether I wanted to turn pro or not, I enlisted in the army in 1963. I spent two years in Alaska, during which time I won several all-military tournaments, and the Alaskan State Amateur.

Just as I was getting used to the cold weather and practicing in snow, I was whisked off to the jungles of Viet Nam, where shooting mortars took the place of shooting golf balls.

I left the service in 1966, then went to work for my dad as an assistant pro at Winged Foot. In 1968 I decided to try to qualify for the PGA Tour.

After qualifying I played on the Tour full time from 1969 to 1971. However, my only high points of this three-year stint were winning the first B.C. Open and playing in two U.S. Open championships. I decided to become a club professional instead and, like my father before me, devote my life to teaching people how to play golf.

Me, practicing golf: the Alaskan way.

I got that "club job," as we pros say. Or rather, that club job came and got me.

To tell this story I have to backtrack in time a few years.

In late 1967, His Royal Majesty King Hassan II of Morocco, after reading *How to Play Golf* by Tommy Armour, expressed an interest in playing what is sometimes called the "royal and ancient pastime." Since kings generally want the very best, and can usually get it at the snap of their fingers, he notified his consulate in America that they were to look Tommy Armour up and bring him back to Morocco to be King Hassan's personal coach.

When Armour received the summons, he wrote a letter back to His Royal Majesty, telling him that he was honored about the invite and happy that his book was so well received. Sadly, however, he couldn't accept the job because he was getting on in years and had stopped traveling. Even the time he could devote to teaching in America was limited.

Here I am, accepting the B.C. Open winner's check, for $2,000.

In that same letter, Armour recommended a "much better teacher." That teacher was my dad.

In 1968, my dad went over to Morocco and got the king started; and in 1969, because I was the first son in my family, I was invited to play in the Moroccan Open at a course just outside Casablanca. As luck would have it, I finished second in the event, which prompted His Majesty to invite me and Julius Boros, two-time U.S. Open champion and 1968 PGA champion, to play golf the next day at his personal nine-hole course, located on the summer palace grounds along the ocean.

On the 3rd hole His Majesty hit his ball into a greenside bunker. After watching him mishit the ball several times, Julius, who was one of the all-time great bunker players, took it upon himself to walk over to His Majesty and give him a quick lesson on hitting the ball out of the trap.

For ten minutes, while His Majesty and Julius were in that trap, all you could see was sand flying up in the air. No ball! Even with Julius's help, the king couldn't hit the ball out of the bunker. Subsequently, he gave up and we continued the round. After completing it, we bowed, then politely said our diplomatic good-byes.

Julius and I drove away in separate chauffeur-driven Mercedes limousines. Then, suddenly, my car was stopped by all the king's men.

"Mr. Harmon, His Majesty would like to know if you could come back and play with him tomorrow," said one of the king's aides.

"Sure, I'd love to, as long as you can have someone change my airline reservations, because I'm scheduled to leave."

"Very well," answered the aide.

"I'll let Julius know," I said, trying to be helpful.

"No, Mr. Boros has some business. He will not be able to make it," said the aide.

I accepted that.

The following day, there we were, the king and I, the only ones playing on his golf course. We played the first two holes and everything was fine; although I thought it kind of fishy that His Majesty hadn't mentioned Mr. Boros at all. On the 3rd hole I found out why.

His Majesty was putting, so I was just standing quietly nearby, not

As fine a sand player as Julius Boros was, he still couldn't help King Hassan II learn how to recover from a bunker.

wanting to disturb his concentration, when I noticed something—or rather didn't notice something—that shocked me.

The sand trap that His Majesty couldn't hit out of the day before had been filled in and sodded, with plants and pretty flowers growing out of the new bright-green grass.

When His Majesty looked up and saw me staring in wonderment at the spot, he looked me straight in the eye and simply said, "Very bad lesson. I didn't want any memories of it."

On my trip to Morocco I visited the city of Rabat with Robert Trent Jones, a famous American golf course architect who was building Royal Dar Es-Salaam, a new 45-hole complex, for His Royal Majesty King Hassan II.

This project was only in the early construction stages, but I was asked if I'd like to be the golf pro when it was completed. Not to be disrespectful to a monarch, I said, "Sure," not thinking anything of it.

Two years later, about November 1971, the Tour was winding down and I was considering taking a club job, somewhere when I got a call from the palace.

"We're ready for you," said the aide.

"Ready for me for what?" I asked with perplexity in my voice.

"To be our pro. You said you would accept the job when the course was ready. Now it's ready," said the aide, referring to the completion of Royal Dar Es-Salaam.

I remember getting off the phone and calling my wife, Lillie. This is how that conversation went:

"Honey, how's your French?"

"Not too bad," she said.

"Good, get packed because we're moving to Morocco. I've accepted the job to be the head pro at Royal Dar Es-Salaam, and the personal teacher to His Royal Majesty King Hassan II of Morocco and the Moroccan Royal Family."

Two weeks later we were in North Africa. So you see, the club job got me—I didn't get it.

I was King Hassan's full-time personal teacher—always by his side, at home or while traveling for the day, via a converted Royal Air Moroccan jet, to places like Paris or other continental destinations.

The fact that His Majesty's picture was on all the money confirmed his importance. However, it took a couple more experiences to see what *special* really meant in Morocco.

One day I was giving the king a lesson in a tent equipped with fans to keep us cool in the sweltering heat. So as not to let too much hot air in, the front flap of the tent was turned up just high enough for the balls to fly out, but not high enough for me or the king to see the direction the balls took. Consequently, the king couldn't tell if he was hitting slices, hooks, shanks, pushes, or sky shots.

I explained to His Majesty that I didn't want to teach this way. I told him that I like to teach "off the ball"—meaning that, for the student's benefit, I relate the curvature of a shot to a particular shape of swing. That way, the student is able to understand how a certain type of swing path (e.g., in-to-out, out-to-in) can create a particular kind of shot (e.g., duck hook, push slice). In short, I made it clear to the king that in order for him to improve on his 20 handicap, he needed to see the flight of the ball.

"That will be arranged, Claude," said the king.

The next day when we drove up, I couldn't believe my eyes. I thought Ringling Brothers, Barnum and Bailey Circus had moved into town. The tent was so big that the King could now hit full shots in it without reaching the other side. And he didn't have to worry about one of his sky shots hitting the top of the tent. The ceiling was around 75 feet high.

"No wonder this guy's picture is on all the money!" I thought to myself.

Another time, His Majesty asked me to arrange for Lee Trevino to come to Morocco to join him in a game of golf. That request was, of course, taken care of, with Lee honored to play with the king (and I).

On the day of our game, Lee and I drove through the gates of the palace. Lee couldn't believe his eyes. The king showed up to greet us for a game of golf with Shetland ponies and dogs by his side. Moreover, before he reached us, he was kissed on the palm and back of each hand by generals and colonels.

Lee could only stand there and say, "Butchie, this is out of a movie. What do I do?"

"Just stand there and wait for him to come over," I said.

After His Majesty formally greeted "Buck" (as Trevino is familiarly known to his best friends), he stepped into a big room with one chair in the middle and more than fifty pairs of golf shoes lining the walls. After one of his aides slipped a pair that matched his attire on his feet, we were on our way.

Lee was so nervous, it took him a few minutes to settle into his opening tee shot. Once we left the tee, I gave him just one bit of advice, so as to avoid another "Boros incident." I told him, "Lee, no matter how bad the king swings, no matter how far he hits the ball off line, no matter how many putts he misses, only help him if you're asked."

The way things went on the 2nd hole, a par three, was indicative of how things were to go the entire day. According to the scorecard, hole number 2 was 140 yards. For this distance, Trevino usually hits a 9-iron. Lee didn't think the hole looked like 140 yards, so he asked, "Butch, how far is this?"

His Majesty said, "Hit an iron five."

Just to accommodate the king and make him feel like he had clubbed Lee perfectly, Lee hit a 5-iron on the green, even though he had to take 40 yards off the shot by swinging much easier than normal. Again and again this happened. Lee, who has a great sense of humor, got a real kick out of that.

During my stay in Morocco as the king's personal teacher, I used the general teaching advice and swing guidelines my father had passed on to me. They worked wonders. In the period of November 1971 to April 1975, I chopped the king's handicap from "20-something" down to 7, which was probably why the king then retained me on a part-time basis. Each winter, until 1980, I returned to Morocco to help His Majesty King Hassan II with his game.

When I left my full-time job as the king's teacher, I took a head pro job at the Crow Valley Golf Club in Iowa.

In 1978 I won the Iowa Match Play Championship. However, I couldn't be lured back to the Tour; teaching had become too much a part of me. In 1979, while in exile, the Shah and Empress of Iran appointed me as their personal teacher.

During the next decade, I worked for a course design and construction company under former PGA champion Dave Marr, accepted a job as golf director at the Bayou Golf Club in Texas City, Texas, opened the

The Shah of Iran (*left*) being taught by me (*center*) and my dad (*right*).

Harmon Golf School, and did trick shot exhibitions. In fact, nothing all that significant happened, until 1989, when my dad died. This was the saddest time of my life. But not long after the mourning period was over, I was, once again, blessed by fate. This time, rather than having a king for a student, I had Davis Love III, one of the PGA Tour's longest hitters.

Like me, Davis was the son of a domineering father who was a big name in the golf business, the late Davis Love, Jr. I had never really met the younger Love before, and how we got together in a teacher-student relationship in 1990 is an interesting story.

I was traveling to Japan with Jeff Sluman, the 1988 PGA champion, who was going there to play in a tournament. Davis, who was on this same trip, joined Jeff and me for dinner after 36 holes of the 72-hole event had been played. When he arrived, he wasn't happy with his game; he had shot 145, and was lying practically dead last after the cut.

We were casually sipping a few Japanese beers afterward, when Jeff asked me if I could help Davis. I turned to Davis and told him that I thought I knew what was wrong with his swing—that it was too long and too steep—and that I'd be glad to work with him upon his return to the States. To my surprise, Davis asked if I could come out and work with him in the morning. He explained to me that normally he would never allow a teacher to give him a formal lesson before a tournament round. I could understand that, because when you get on the course the last thing you want is a dozen swing thoughts swimming around in your head. In this case, however, Davis was so frustrated with the blocked shots he was hitting, and felt he was playing so badly, that he had nothing to lose and all to gain. That was enough for me to agree to meet him on the practice tee the next day after breakfast.

I told Davis to visualize a baseball batter's horizontal swing. Then, I had him hit shots off gentle sidehill lies, with the ball above his feet, to help him flatten his overly steep swing plane. His exaggerated upright plane, particularly, was causing him to hit weak, off-line shots.

I told myself as I worked with him that this is what Dad would have done. In fact, in my mind I could hear him saying, "Butch, when you're teaching someone, always get rid of the cancer first; that way, the student will hit better shots right away and regain his or her confidence quickly. Also, the other elements of the swing that were off track will fall back into place."

Well, with his new swing, Davis shot 131 the next two rounds and moved way up the leader board. We've been linked up ever since.

It's very satisfying to say that since I've taught Davis, he's won several big events, including the 1992 Tournament Players Championship (which many golf aficionados consider to be the "fifth major"), the 1992 MCI Heritage Classic, the 1993 Infinity Tournament of Champions, the 1993 Las Vegas Invitational, the 1995 New Orleans Open, and the 1996 Buick Invitational. Davis also finished second in the 1995 Masters, an accomplishment we both recognize as something special.

Still, the student I'm most proud of is Greg Norman. That's not because he's made such great strides since coming to me for lessons in late 1991, after finishing 53rd on the PGA Tour's money list. I'm impressed with Greg because he had the courage to face up to his weaknesses and do something to improve. He could have stuck with his game and probably won a few tournaments along the way. Not Greg. He is such a dedicated and determined individual that he was willing to make some major changes in his swing, pitching technique, and putting stroke to get to the level he is at today.

Only Ben Hogan before him, who worked extra hard to change a duck hook swing to a power fade swing, and Nick Faldo, who totally revamped his swing, have shown such courage. You can learn about the will to win and the definition of hard work on the practice tee by looking at what these guys had to go through to become the players they have been.

When Greg first started working with me, he told me that he wanted most to stop blocking drives and spinning pitch shots.

In his pitches, Greg was imparting so much spin to the ball that his shots would tend to land by the pin or just beyond it, back up off the green, then roll into the heavy fringe grass. Consequently, he was missing a lot of birdie opportunities, something you can't afford to do on the PGA Tour where the competition is the toughest in the world.

Later on, Greg asked me to help him solve a putting problem.

We worked long and hard to fix his problems (something I'll explain later in the book). These days, Greg hits a lot more fairways and greens, and sinks many more putts, owing to the subtle changes made in his long- and short-game techniques. He's the first to admit that practice does, indeed, pay off. All you have to do is look at his record since we joined forces in late 1991.

Ben Hogan has taught golfers, including pros Greg Norman and Nick Faldo, the value of hard, honest practice.

In 1992 he finished eighteenth on the money list.

In 1993 he ranked third at the close of the season.

In 1994 he came in second by a whisker to Nick Price, earning $1,330,307 to Price's $1,499,927. However, Norman's entire game improved. His scoring average of 68.81 was lower than any other pro's on the PGA Tour.

In 1995 his scoring average was still the lowest on the PGA Tour. He came in first on the money list and he won Player of the Year honors as well—a truly tremendous effort.

During that four-year stretch, Greg won some big events, including the 1992 Canadian Open, the 1993 Doral Open, the 1993 British Open, the 1994 Tournament Players Championship (shooting a record 24 under par score of 264 at TPC Sawgrass in Ponte Vedra Beach, Florida), the 1995 Memorial, and the 1995 World Series of Golf.

Tiger Woods is my most recent "celebrity" student, and it's hard to determine which is bigger, his dedication or his potential.

I started teaching Tiger in 1993. Tiger had lost in the second round of that year's U.S. Amateur championship. The previous year, Tiger lost

Two of my top pro students, Greg Norman (*left*) and Davis Love (*right*).

in the same round, and in 1991 he failed to qualify for the match play. His father, Earl, called me to ask if I could take a look at Tiger's swing and make some suggestions. He wanted to stop whatever it was that was preventing his son from playing to his full potential.

Tiger, like Love and Norman, is tall, so he naturally has a tendency to set the wrists too early. This problem causes the club to dip well beyond the parallel position at the top, thereby hindering control of the swing. Furthermore, the arc of the swing narrows, causing vital power to be lost.

Another problem Tiger had when he came to me for lessons was letting his right foot rise up too early and much too high prior to impact. This fault ultimately caused him to hit either a push to the right of the target or a snap hook well left of the target, depending on how fast he could release his hands and arms.

Standing up, as I call it, before impact prevents you from shifting your weight fully to your left side and clearing your left hip out of the way. Consequently, the tendency is to hit either a push shot that flies well right of the target or a snap hook that darts left the second it leaves the clubface.

Fortunately, Tiger is very athletic and worked the problems out in a very short time; in fact, to such a degree that he started playing pro-style golf in 1994. His biggest win that year was the United States Amateur championship—a tournament that he won again in 1995.

In helping all three of these players iron out their faults, I couldn't help but think of how far I had come since age 8, when I gave my first golf lesson to my brother Craig. I was proud of myself for persevering and taking pride in teaching golf. Furthermore, I couldn't help but think how much credit I owed to my father.

In teaching Norman, Love, and Woods, I found myself teaching them a lot of the same things my father taught me: namely, to know where the clubface is at all times during the swing; to bump the left hip toward the target before clearing it; and to let the heel of the right foot lead the toe end when shifting weight to your left side on the downswing.

That made me feel good, because Dad always believed in passing on what he learned.

In Chapter Four, I'll describe in great detail the changes I made to the techniques of Dave Love III, Greg Norman, and Tiger Woods. You'll be surprised how similar their errors are to yours. Just by studying the photographs and reading the accompanying instruction, you'll learn quite a bit about how to improve your own game.

But before you do that, I want to teach you the building blocks, or fundamentals, that are needed for improving your scores and enjoying the game for a long time to come.

The Four Cornerstones

of Winning Golf

BALL STRIKING,

SHORT GAME,

MENTAL SIDE/COURSE MANAGEMENT,

AND PHYSICAL CONDITIONING

I'd like to begin this very extensive chapter by telling you a little bit about what it's like to teach the game of golf as one's life work. This might sound a little corny, and I know I'm prejudiced, but I believe that being a golf instructor is one of the most fascinating and rewarding roles any person could have. I wouldn't trade my job for anyone's.

Whenever I meet a new student, we have an automatic bond right off the bat, in that we share a love and respect for the game of golf. I wouldn't be in my position as the instructor if I didn't. And they wouldn't be coming to see me if they didn't have a sincere interest in learning how to play enjoyable golf.

I know how much it means to most golfers to advance their overall game to a new level or to learn how to play a certain shot that has baffled them for as long as they've played the game. Say, for example, I'm working with students who have just never managed to grasp the key points that will allow them to play bunker shots successfully. When they step into a greenside bunker, they do so with a sense of despair, knowing they'll probably take at least two shots to get out, maybe more, or that they'll wind up picking the ball up and taking an "X" on the hole. When I get a bad bunker player to finally use the correct swing motion through impact, and the ball pops up and out of the sand nice and softly, and then the student repeats the shot enough times to know that he or she has finally "got it"—well, it's a very gratifying feeling. It's as if I had just taught my own child how to ride a two-wheeled bike without training wheels; it's a milestone that we both can take joy and pride in.

I meant what I said in the subhead to Chapter One: I don't teach golf; I teach "people how to play golf." There's a difference between "teaching golf" and teaching each individual student the best way for him or her to *play* golf.

You see, some teachers believe that there are definite sets of rules regarding the setup and the full swing, about the type of flight you should produce on all your shots, about the one way to play chip shots, about the "right" way to putt. In other words, these teachers believe they have a *formula* by which every individual must swing the club and, indeed, play the game.

Well, it's fine to sit around and discuss theories about what the elements of the perfect swing or the perfect putting stroke are. It's easy to say that everyone should strive to swing the club like Sam Snead, and then you'll be an outstanding player. But to me, trying to tell all students how they *must* swing and how they *must* play shots doesn't mean I'm doing a great job of teaching. It's impractical to try to teach everyone the perfect swing. And if there's one thing I do in working with my students, it's teach them a *practical* approach to playing golf to the very best of their personal, physical ability.

In my career I've given lessons to thousands upon thousands of golfers. I teach some golfers who are outstanding athletes, with Greg Norman at the top of that list. I teach far more golfers who have just fair athletic ability and coordination, and many also who, quite honestly, are poor athletes. I teach golfers who have the opportunity to play and practice four or five times a week. I teach golfers whose other demands and priorities mean that they'll only get to the golf course a dozen times per year. I teach tall golfers, short golfers, overweight golfers, skinny golfers, elderly golfers who have reduced strength and physical range of motion, juniors who are still growing mentally as well as physically, golfers who've worked hard on swing theory with good instructors for twenty years or more, and many more who have never had a lesson. How can I teach everyone the same way? How can I assume everyone has the same ability to grasp a certain level of instruction? How, even more importantly, can I assume that everyone can make the same physical moves I am dictating to them as key elements of the golf swing? Through the wise guidance of my dad, and through an even better teacher—my own experience—I have learned that I can't just teach golf. I have to teach people how to play golf.

My goal is to take each student individually and, given the framework of his or her current level of ability, develop a practical approach that will allow the golfers to make the most of their own physical and mental package, help them both swing the golf club and play the game the best they can. As far as the golf swing is concerned, my goal is to teach golfers some important basics of the setup and the swing, and to get them to gradually build a swinging action they can depend on. Again, going back to their own physical characteristics, after working with me it's highly unlikely that they'll immediately develop a technically picture-perfect swing; but I'm confident that I'll be able to teach them a relatively effective, efficient golf swing in a surprisingly short time.

Perhaps more important than the quality of the swing itself (and I realize that this sounds a little funny because most golf students seem to think that the golf swing is the only thing that's important), is learning how to play the game of golf; in other words, the art of scoring in golf. Let me give you an analogy.

If you've ever spent time in a basketball gym, perhaps at a local college, you've probably seen guys practicing their shooting, usually long jump shots, and boy, do they ever look impressive. From 20, 25, even 30 feet out, they're nailing those jump shots one after the other. Maybe one guy is a member of the local college team; and if you enjoy basketball you might say, I'd like to see how this guy does in competition. I wonder why I haven't recognized him or seen his name in the paper—he looks like he could score at least 20 points with his eyes closed.

Well, if you do happen to see that team play, you might be surprised to notice that that same hot-shot shooter isn't even a starter on the team. When he does get into the game he doesn't seem to get a lot done, maybe doesn't even score, doesn't even get off a single one of those long-range bombs. The next day you look at a box score and wonder, how could a guy who looks so great not even be a factor when it comes to actually playing the game?

Whether it's in basketball or in golf, there's a big difference between just being a shooter and being a scorer. More important even than a basketball player's ability to shoot, is his ability to get himself into position to score. The same is true for the golfer. There are thousands, maybe millions, of players who have great-looking golf swings, who are able to hit great-looking shots. But there are not nearly as many who maximize the level of shotmaking skills they possess and shoot the best possible score.

Building a Better Game
Through the Four Cornerstones of Winning Golf

All of the above is not to say that, if your current average score is 100, you're never going to improve very much, that you should be content to maximize what you have and get your scores, perhaps, into the low to mid-90s. Maybe in the short term that is what I'll try to help you accomplish. However, golfers who come to me for help will also learn about what it takes to truly maximize their ability as golfers for the rest of their lives. This brings me to the real key to my approach as a teacher: The Four Cornerstones of Winning Golf.

It's interesting that so many amateurs, when they think of improving their games, think of only one thing: improving their golf swing. Sure, it's great to develop a technically sound golf swing and to hit the ball higher, longer, and straighter than before. However, the golfer who accomplishes this has improved in only one out of the four areas needed in order to become a complete player. The four cornerstones that make up the game of golf are as follows:

Ball Striking
Short Game
Mental Side/Course Management
Physical Conditioning

If you are spending every minute that you work on your golf game simply trying to improve your swing, you are working on only one aspect of the game and ignoring the rest. Therefore you can expect only limited improvement in your overall game. Let's take a look at the four cornerstones of golf and see how each one contributes equally to your success as a golfer.

BALL STRIKING

Certainly, you want to develop a swing that allows you to drive the ball a reasonable distance and keep it in the fairway a high percentage of the time. And you'd like to feel confident that you will hit the green with your irons more often than not. Good ball striking makes the game more predictable. If you never stray too far from the fairways and greens, you're not likely to incur penalty strokes or play shots from under trees or from terrible lies, so you're not likely to take those triple bogeys that send a round into a tailspin. Sure, it's a great goal to try to improve the consistency of your shotmaking.

Still, striking the ball better does not make you a complete golfer, nor does good ball striking guarantee that you'll shoot a low score. Yes, good ball striking, combined with a well-developed short game, combined with a great mental approach to the game and refined course management skills, and combined with improved physical conditioning, will make you the best player you can be. But good ball striking does not stand alone from these other key elements that make up the complete golfer's skills.

Keep this in mind as you plan your practice time in the future. Sure, I'd like you to work on improving your ball striking skills, but doing so should only take up only a certain percentage of your practice time. The rest of your practice time should be spent on developing your short game, your mental side and course management skills, and your physical conditioning.

SHORT GAME

If you think about it, you'll realize that you hit more shots in a round of golf from within 75 yards of the hole than you do from outside 75 yards. It sounds incredible, but it's true. For the everyday golfer, let's say a golfer who's a little better than the national average and shoots 90, the following tabulation illustrates how a round is likely to break down. (All shots in the short game, which includes putting, are shown in bold type.)

Shotmaking Category	Average Strokes Per Round
Tee shots, par 4s and 5s	14
Tee shots, par 3s	4
Second shots, par 4s and 5s	14
Third shots, par 5s (longer than 75 yards)	3
"Recovery" shots longer than 75 yards	3
Penalty strokes	2
Recovery pitch shots, 20–75 yards	**6**
Third shots, par 5s (shorter than 75 yards)	**1**
Chip shots, greenside to 20 yards	**5**
Sand shots	**3**
Putts	**35**
Total strokes	90
Total short game shots	**50**

So you see, in the course of an average round of 90, the average number of strokes involved in the short game or putting is 50—more than half the number of total strokes for the round!

Based on this, you might reasonably ask, why do I rate ball striking and the short game of equal importance to the total game of golf if short game strokes make up more of the round? Well, I think you should also take into consideration the fact that, of the 35 putts the average golfer may take during a round, a good percentage that actually go into the hole—let's say 10—are virtual tap-ins of two feet or less. These usually occur after the first putt is missed by a small amount (while some unfortunately come after the second putt is missed, but sometimes also after an excellent chip or short approach). I don't think you can give equal weight to tap-in putts and all the other shots. Figuring in this factor, then, full-swing shots and short-game shots carry about equal weight.

MENTAL SIDE/COURSE MANAGEMENT

You could successfully argue that no one in the history of golf has ever hit a shot with the mental side of the game. You can't make the ball move with your mind. However, your mental approach to every shot you hit—which includes your course management skills, your plotting a game plan similar to the way a chess master plans moves in advance—has a great deal more to do with the outcome of a shot than you'd ever imagine. I will talk about the mental side in greater detail later. However, let me say here that I have never in my teaching career met a truly great player who approached the game, or even a single shot, with a negative or haphazard mental outlook. When you think of the greatest players of the past forty years or so—Arnold Palmer, Jack Nicklaus, Gary Player, Tom Watson, Lee Trevino, Greg Norman, Nick Faldo—could anyone begin to suggest that any of these golfers play the game without an enormously strong mental approach? All of these golfers have thrived when the pressure was the greatest—that's why their records are so phenomenal. And I believe that they thrive on the pressure situations that cause lesser golfers to falter, precisely because the mental side of their game has been that much stronger than their competition's. I believe that average golfers can do as much to improve the mental side of the game (and with it, their course management skills) as they can in any area of the mechanics of the game.

PHYSICAL CONDITIONING

Okay, golfers, the fourth cornerstone of winning golf is the one that I am sure a lot of you are not going to want to hear about—which is exactly why you need to hear about it. And that's physical conditioning. A good physical condition is the last piece necessary for a good, solid game.

Don't ever let anyone tell you that good execution of the golf swing is not an outstanding athletic achievement. For a golfer to make a swinging motion with a 44-inch driver, in which he or she generates over 100 miles per hour of clubhead speed at impact, and delivers that clubhead in such a way that the clubface is traveling perfectly along the target line as it makes impact (which is what is necessary to make a tee shot fly 260 yards or more right down the middle)—well, that is a tremendous physical feat. It is a great combination of athletic precision and power. So are well-played iron shots. So are putts, believe it or not, where your sensory awareness as well as your perfect steadiness through the stroke are crucial to your success.

Last, and this has been proven time and again by medical research, your mental approach is definitely affected by your physical conditioning. It's easy to say you should be mentally sharp in your approach to the psychological challenges of the game, but if you're not in shape physically, you're just not going to be in strong mental shape either. We will go into this in detail later in this chapter, of course. For now, please trust me when I say that if you improve your physical conditioning, you will improve both the physical and mental sides of your golf game.

Now that you know the four cornerstones of winning golf—ball striking, short game, mental side/course management, and physical conditioning—let's spend some time breaking down these key areas and showing you how you can improve within each area of the total golf package.

Ball Striking — The Setup Governs the Swing

I'm sure you know the feeling: you're at your home course, or any course for that matter, waiting your turn at the first tee watching people tee off, when you find yourself watching a player getting ready to hit and you think, "This guy looks like he can play." You've spotted something about the player's preparatory moves prior to swinging that tells you he's going to hit a good shot.

What you have spotted in this golfer, although you don't quite know how to put it into words, is an excellent, athletic setup position. A good golf swing and consistent ball striking are almost always the result of the solid foundation of a good setup. So let me try to put into words what this good athletic setup entails.

The setup position: front view.

The first thing I want to tell you about the setup is something Dad made certain I understood during my own formative years as a golfer: The first move in setting up to a full golf shot is to lay the clubface down behind the ball, pointing it squarely at your target. You then build your entire setup around that square clubface. *The ideal goal of the setup is to put your body in a position that will allow you to swing the club correctly, and return it to that same square position it was in when you first set it down on the ground behind the ball.*

In a way, talking about the setup is like talking about what automobile manufacturers call the "ergonomics" of car design. Basically, they're saying that they design the car to fit around your body's needs. In the same way, you set yourself up around the golf club so that you will conform to its need to contact the ball squarely.

THE "STRONG" GRIP

Okay, you have laid that clubface down squarely behind the back of the ball. Now it's time to secure your hold on the club.

First, lay the club diagonally across the fingers and palm of the left hand, so that it runs on a line from across the top joint of your forefinger down across the middle of your heel pad. Next, close your left hand over the club. As you look down, you should be able to clearly see the top knuckles of the first two fingers of your left hand, and you should also see part or all of the top knuckle of your ring finger as well. As you close your left hand around the handle, the left thumb must lie down the right side of the grip. This position of the left thumb is, I believe, one of the most significant points about the grip. When your left thumb is on the right side of the shaft, the space or V formed by your thumb and forefinger points to the right of a "straight-up" position. In your completed setup, this V should point just to the right of your right ear or to the inside of your right shoulder.

The correct left-hand grip.

This position of the left hand is referred to as a "strong" position. A "weak" position, by comparison, is one in which the left thumb is pointing directly down the center of the shaft. This would mean that as you look down, you would see only one knuckle of the left hand, as opposed to two or three, and that the

V formed by the thumb and forefinger would point straight up at your chin, rather than toward the inside of the right shoulder.

At this point I'd better explain precisely what is meant by the terms *strong* and *weak*. A strong grip is one in which both hands are turned relatively more to the right on the club handle, while the clubface is aligned squarely to the target. A weak grip is one in which both hands are turned relatively more to the left on the handle while the clubface is aligned squarely.

With the hands turned more to the right, in a strong grip, the golfer is more apt to arrive at the top with his left wrist in a cupped position. From here, however, it becomes a lot easier for the golfer to return the club back to a square position at impact or to even close the clubface a little so that the ball draws from right to left. So, if you like a strong grip, don't try to establish a flat left wrist position at the top. Maintain the cupped position.

The term *strong* comes from the fact that, historically, the right-to-left draw has been considered a stronger shot than the fade or slice.

Conversely, when the left hand is placed on the club in a *weak* position with the left thumb down the top of the shaft, it becomes more difficult for the golfer to get the clubface back to square in the impact zone. The tendency is to bring the club back into the ball with the clubface a bit more open in relation to the target line, so that the shot fades to the right.

By the way, the terms *strong* and *weak* have nothing to do with the amount of force you use to hold the club (something we'll talk about a little later). They refer strictly to the relative position of the hands on the grip of the club.

Now that you've got your left-hand grip in position, let's talk about the right hand and the manner in which the hands mesh together.

If you've played golf for a while, you've probably heard of the "overlapping" and "interlocking" grips, as well as the ten-finger grip. The terms *overlapping* and *interlocking* refer to the manner in which the right little, or pinkie, finger links itself with the left hand on the club.

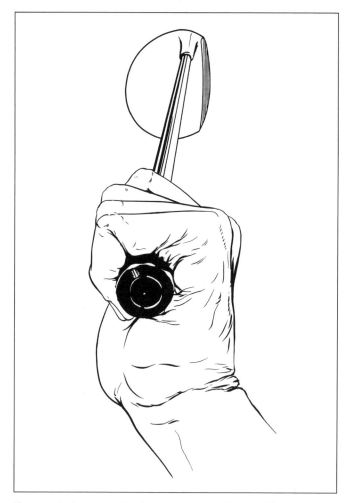

If your grip is strong, it's okay to arrive in a "cupped" position at the top of the swing.

In the overlapping grip, the right little finger overlaps or rests in the crease between the index finger and middle finger of the left hand. In the interlocking grip, instead of laying the right little finger on top, you actually slide it underneath your left index finger, so that it and the left index finger intertwine. In the ten-finger grip, all the fingers of the left and right hands lie directly on the club handle.

While for most golfers I don't recommend the use of the ten-finger grip, it shouldn't be completely dismissed as a viable hold on the club. After all, Art Wall, Jr., won the Masters in 1959 using a ten-finger grip. The ten-finger grip, however, is probably better suited to beginners and juniors, because it encourages lively hand action by the very fact that the right hand is completely on the handle. As most players advance to the point of needing to gain control more than distance, they will probably benefit from a move to the overlap or the interlock position.

OVERLAPPING VS. INTERLOCKING IS *NOT* THE KEY TO A GOOD GRIP

You hear so much about overlapping or interlocking these fingers, you'd think that whichever one of these grips you choose is crucial. It's not. Overlapping versus interlocking is not what's truly important about a grip. It's the overall positioning of the hands in relation to the club handle that counts. True, the majority of better golfers use the overlapping position. But there have been a large enough number of great players,

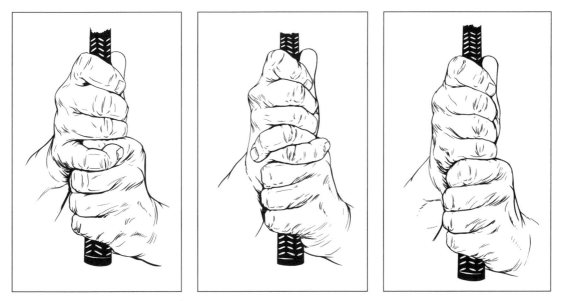

(*Left to right*) The overlapping grip; the interlocking grip; the ten-finger grip.

headed by Jack Nicklaus and Tom Kite, who have used an interlocking grip, that it would be unreasonable to discourage anyone from using it.

While I'm on the subject, you might find it interesting that Greg Norman uses a rare variation of the interlock grip. Instead of completely intertwining his right pinkie with his left index finger, Norman actually presses the end of his pinkie into the web between the left index and middle fingers. Greg refers to this position as his "intermesh" grip, and feels it's an even more secure and comfortable variation of the standard interlock grip. I think this just goes to show that exactly how you connect the hands is more a matter of personal preference than it is a key to shot-making. Overlapping versus interlocking is somewhat a choice based on trial and error. While, as I said, the overlap is the more prevalent style, many golfers whose hands are relatively small seem to prefer the security that the interlocking of the fingers brings them. Really, the choice is yours.

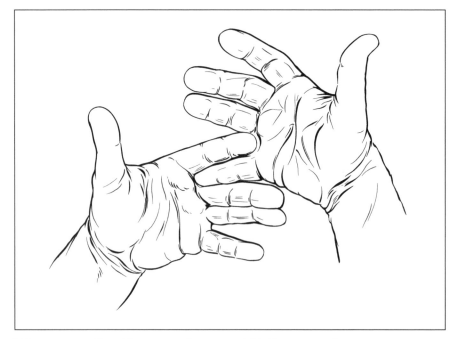

When gripping, Greg Norman prefers to mesh his fingers together.

But back to the complete positioning of the right hand on the club. Once you have overlapped or interlocked that right little finger, your remaining three fingers should be underneath the handle of the club. Close them gently, then wrap the palm of your right hand over your left thumb, which is already positioned on the right side of the grip. The pad of your right hand should press down slightly on the top part of your left thumb. Having closed the right hand, your right thumb should rest lightly against the left side of the club handle, with the V formed by your right thumb and forefinger pointing to the inside of your right shoulder.

It's interesting to note that after a number of years in which the weak grip position was in vogue, the strong position has made a real comeback, even with the Tour pros. Most teachers would argue that the better player you are, the less likely you are to need a strong grip position. The pros, who play every day and generate great clubhead speed, should have no trouble squaring up the clubface, and, if anything, they would want a grip that makes it harder for them to hook the ball. Conversely, it had been argued in the past that the strong grip position was something of a crutch that was okay for use by poorer golfers who sliced the ball, since this grip helped the slicer keep the clubface squarer to the target line.

Well, time has proven that the relatively strong grip position I have described works best for most golfers, right from superstars such as Fred Couples down to the everyday weekend amateur. And I think there's a little-known advantage to this hold on the club: The strong grip contributes positively to a good backswing because when you use it, the left arm is tilted somewhat clockwise at address. Without getting too far ahead of myself, this position means the left arm is ready to rotate the clubhead in a clockwise manner on the backswing, which leads to the desirable, relatively shallow swing path through the ball that we'll talk about later.

THOUGHTS ON GRIP PRESSURE

My thoughts differ from many other teachers' in regard to how much pressure you should use to grip the club and as to where those par-

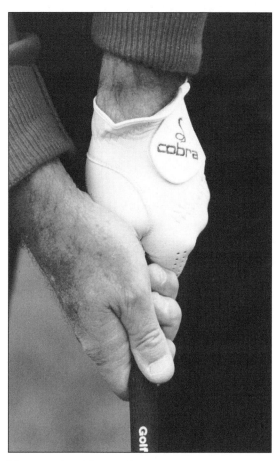

In gripping the club, the pad of the right hand should lightly "squeeze" the left thumb.

The completed "strong" grip position.

ticular pressure points should be. I believe that the degree of pressure should be equal for all the fingers as well as the palms. This may be in contrast to what you have heard elsewhere. Despite what you've heard, I believe your hands will mesh best as a team if you put equal pressure on the club not only with each hand, but with each finger.

You also hear, quite frequently, that you should grip the club as lightly as possible. Common images are that you should hold the golf club as you would hold a bird, or as if you were squeezing toothpaste out of a full tube. I believe these images represent too light a grip pressure. I recommend that you grip the club for normal shots so that you feel a slight tension in your forearms and wrists—not to the point of being rigid, but to where there is some tension. Although this is pretty much a subjective judgment, if you would call holding something as lightly as you can a rating of "1" for grip pressure, and holding something as tightly as you can a "10," then I suggest a grip pressure of 6 to 7 for most full shots.

It's important to note that this image might change just a little from one golfer to the next. If you happen to be a dock loader and your hands and forearms are very strong because of the nature of your work, your hold can probably feel pretty light, yet still be secure. Conversely, if you play little golf and do nothing else in particular to build up your hands and forearms, you might need to hold the club somewhat tighter. The more you play and hit balls, the more strength you'll automatically develop in your hands.

You should also be aware that grip pressure should change for certain types of specialized shots. For example, if you're trying to hit a low punch shot into a strong wind, and you want to lead the clubhead through impact with the hands, you'll need to hang onto the club pretty tightly—maybe an 8 or 9 on your personal pressure scale. On the other hand, if you're trying to loft a soft lob shot over a bunker and stop it near a tight pin, you need light pressure, maybe a 3 in both hands. In general, if you want to hit the ball low, tighten your grip, and if you want to hit a high, soft shot, grip the club lightly.

To sum up our discussion of the grip: if you have been holding the club in some other fashion than what I've described, practice developing the holds I've explained here. You may be pleasantly surprised to find that these grips are not as terribly uncomfortable as you might expect them to be. They will definitely be more comfortable to you if, until now, you have been struggling to grip the club with your hands in a weak position.

STANCE: PARALLEL LEFT AND WIDE

As I stated earlier, you want to develop your setup by building it around your clubface, which you align square to the target. Your goal is to develop a setup for all full shots in which your body is aligned parallel left of your target. A lot of golfers misinterpret what parallel left means, so let me make sure you understand it.

The "parallel left" address position.

For all full shots, you want to get into a position in which a line across, not only your toes, but your knees, hips, and shoulders would run parallel left of the target line. Visualize a railroad track on which the club-face and the ball lie directly on the outside rail, and your target also lies on that outside rail in the distance. Your toes should run along the inside track of that railroad track, with your knees, hips and shoulders also running directly along the inside track line. If the line along these body parts pointed directly at the target that's on the outside rail, it would actually mean you are aimed a shade to the right of the target. If you frequently hit good shots to the green but miss slightly to the right, it could be that you've simply been misaligning in that direction.

Greg Norman has a beautiful method of working into his stance, one that every golfer would do well to copy. Starting from behind the ball, Norman walks around the ball to his left, placing his right foot into a position behind the ball and perpendicular to his target line. Next, after positioning the clubhead carefully behind the ball, Norman sets himself up to the golf club. He then places his left foot down, so that both feet are aligned parallel left of the target line. However, the toe end of his left foot is fanned out, perhaps 20 degrees, instead of being perpendicular to the line. Next, Norman spreads his right foot backward, about 4 to 6 inches back of where he had originally placed it, and turns that toe out a touch also (but not quite as much as the left toe).

You frequently hear it said that the golfer should have his or her feet placed at about shoulder width for a driver, but really, that directive is a little vague. I'd like to see every golfer strive for a stance that has the insides of the heels at least as wide as the shoulders for a driver, and then narrow down gradually from there. Appreciate the fact that I emphasized the word *gradually*. That's because I believe most golfers will benefit from having a stance that's a bit on the wide side rather than one that is too narrow. The golf swing is an athletic movement, and as in most other sports, a relatively wide stance gives you the base you need to make a full swing, yet stay well balanced throughout.

Your weight distribution should be such that your weight rests on the balls of the feet, rather than on the toes or the heels. An important part of solid ball striking is that you hold your position in space throughout the swing, neither rocking back on your heels nor falling forward toward the ball.

For most full shots, you should feel that 50 percent of your weight is on your left foot and 50 percent is on your right as you prepare to hit. Only on certain shorter shots, such as a punched short iron or for chip shots, should you feel as though your weight is balanced more on your left side.

BALL POSITION: STAY FAIRLY CONSTANT

I'd like to spend a minute here clarifying a confusing part of the setup to many amateurs: namely, the ball's position in the stance.

Quite often you'll hear that ball position can vary in your stance, anywhere from opposite your left instep to opposite a point right of center of your stance (for a right-handed player). Described this way, the ball's position could vary as much as 10 inches from the driver through the wedge.

I don't believe the ball's position should change that much. In fact, I

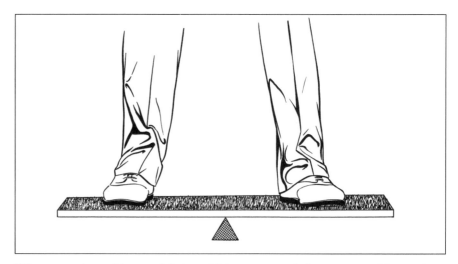

When preparing to hit most full shots, it's important to balance your weight evenly on the ball of each foot.

This ball position works well for most shots, including the driver, shown here.

stick to one basic philosophy: Unless you're playing a specialty shot, such as a running chip or an extra-high pitch, try to play all your shots with the ball positioned opposite your left armpit. This strategy takes the guesswork out of golf. Furthermore, a constant ball position will make you a more consistent player.

I might add that ball position is a bit of an illusion to begin with; it does not vary as much as people think. You see, when your stance is fairly wide, as with a driver, the ball looks as though it's a lot more forward in your stance than it does with, say, a 9-iron. While the ball is a bit farther back with the 9-iron, it looks as though it is even farther back, because at the same time your stance has become narrower. What actually happens is that your right foot is now closer to the left and, therefore, also closer to a line drawn to the ball.

Ball position is an important factor because it has a two-dimensional effect on your shots. If the ball is too far back in your stance, it leads to hitting the ball "thin" or topping it outright, since the club hasn't approached its lowest point. If the ball is too far forward, you'll have a tendency to catch the ground first, hitting it "fat." What many golfers don't realize, though, is that incorrect ball placement can affect their aim as well. When the ball is too far back in the stance, your shoulder alignment will automatically close, pointing the right-hander to the right of the target. If you let the ball wander too far forward in your stance, you'll end up reaching for it with your right arm and shoulder, so that your shoulders are open in relation to the target. To avoid these problems, you should keep your ball position fairly constant, at or slightly inside a line drawn to your left heel or left armpit.

BUILDING AN ATHLETIC PRESWING POSTURE

I don't think you can ever underestimate the value of maintaining perfect balance in the golf swing. As my dad pointed out to me many times, the quality of a person's ball striking depends, more than anything else, on his or her ability to deliver the clubhead squarely to the ball. If you don't maintain balance during the swing, you're not going to hit the ball on the "sweet spot" with the consistency you need. So, you need to build good balance into the posture you assume at address.

Once you have stepped into your stance as described earlier, bend forward from your hips, not from your waist, so that your spine is bent forward from an upright position to about 30 degrees. Your rear end will be pushed out and up slightly by this forward bend of the spine. Again, make sure that your weight is on the balls of your feet.

From this body position, let your arms hang naturally. You'll notice that because your spine is tilted forward, your arms will be a short distance, say 6 inches, away from your thighs while hanging naturally. This is perfect. You should not have to reach your arms into position to grip the golf club. Assemble your grip on the club right where the arms hang after you have leaned forward from the hips by that 30-degree angle.

A question I'm often asked is, "How far should I stand from the ball at address, and how will I know if I'm standing at the right distance?" Where your arms hang, as well as the length of the club you are swinging, will tell you how far to stand from the ball. Here's a test: Take your regular stance and grip the club with the clubhead behind the ball. Now take your right hand off the club and let the arm hang freely. Is your right hand just beside where it would rest on the clubshaft? If so, it means your arms are in a natural, relaxed position on the club, and this also means that you're standing the correct distance from the ball. If, however, your right hand hangs closer to your body than it did when you gripped the club, it means you were reaching for the ball at address, and thus standing too far away from it. Conversely, if you're standing too close to the ball, when you take your right hand off the handle you'll see that it naturally hangs farther down the shaft than where you were gripping it.

Of course, the longer the club you're hitting, the farther you'll be standing from the ball. The average driver today, some 44 inches long, is about 8 inches longer than a pitching wedge. So, even though that clubshaft is angled downward toward the ground, it will still extend somewhat outward, so that you'll be farther from the ball with your driver, even though your address posture remains the same.

As a rule, though, many more golfers stand too far away from the ball at address than stand too close to it. Standing too far away pushes you forward, so it's difficult to maintain that all-important balance in the swing. It also puts too much tension in your arms prior to beginning the swing. This right-hand-off-the-club measurement is a good way to be sure that your posture and your distance from the ball at address are as they should be.

One last point about your setup concerns the positioning of your shoulders. If you are right-handed, you are going to grip the club with your right hand just underneath the left on the shaft. This means that your right shoulder should be slightly lower than your left at address. You don't need to think about this too much; just be natural about it, while making sure to keep your shoulders directly on that inside track that points parallel left in relation to your target line.

I suggest that you take advantage of the opportunity to watch Greg Norman set up to the ball whenever you get a chance to see him on television. Greg has always been meticulous about all the factors in the setup that we've discussed. He became even more so later in his career, which is one big reason he has played so well since 1992.

Work hard on your setup routine on the practice tee. You need to make the same preswing moves over and over and over. Step away from that pile of range balls and practice your entire preshot routine with every ball. Setting up well to the ball most of the time isn't good enough. You need to set up the same way every time. If you don't have a sequence of checkpoints for every shot, it's easy for something to get off track; then, when you start missing shots, you won't know why. It's much easier to get your swing back under control if you consciously make certain that your grip, alignment, and posture are all as we've discussed, prior to starting the swing. That said, let's now talk about the bridge between addressing the ball and making that swing.

THE WAGGLE: A DRESS REHEARSAL

If you've played a fair amount of golf to date, you've probably noticed that very few golfers, once they've set up over the ball, simply go ahead and swing back from a dead-still position. Certainly no really good player does this. All good golfers have a preliminary bridging motion between their setup and the beginning of their backswing. This bridging motion is known as the waggle.

To the untrained eye, the motions that make up the waggle (which are often very different from one golfer to the next, I might add) must look like nothing more than nervous fidgeting. The waggle is much more than that. It is an important part of executing the shot—really, a sort of miniature practice swing from which the "real" swing emanates.

My dad emphasized the importance of the waggle to me early on. Dad believed the waggle was an integral part of the swing, I guess, because he played so often with Ben Hogan, in practice and competition. Mr. Hogan was known for having a beautiful preswing waggle. His hands and wrists did most of the work, cocking the club rhythmically upward and away from the ball, then back down to it. As he did this, though, his legs, arms, and torso seemed to pick up the beat from his hands and wrists, so that he was in a constant, albeit slight, motion prior to starting the swing. Most important, perhaps, is the fact that with Mr. Hogan, as with all good players, there is no specific stop to the waggle—instead, the waggle actually blends into the backswing itself.

Dad believed the waggle acted as a preprogrammer of, or precursor to, the swing; in other words, a player tends to swing the club as he or she waggles it. Jack Nicklaus has a fairly long, slow, gentle waggle, with little lifting or cocking of the club with his wrists. And, of course, Nicklaus has always had a very deliberate, body-oriented swing with relatively little visible hand action involved. Arnold Palmer's waggle is a quicker,

One cue that may help you with the transition from a good rhythmic waggle directly into the backswing is a very slight movement known as the *forward press*. This is a movement of either the hands or some other part of the body toward the target, from which the actual motion of the backswing begins.

My dad always admired Ben Hogan's slight forward press, in which his hands moved toward the target just an inch or so after his last waggle, and then he more or less rebounded into his backswing move. Perhaps an even more obvious forward press is the one used by Gary Player. Player kicks his right knee inward, toward the target, and then recoils from this move directly into his backswing.

This triggering cue does not necessarily even need to be a movement toward the target. Jack Nicklaus, for example, rotates his chin to the right, then pushes the club back immediately following this ready cue. Whatever the movement happens to be, the important thing is that there is a movement that triggers the start of your backswing, rather than your starting it from a stock-still position. As you practice your waggle, see if developing a forward press suits you as well.

more staccato type of movement, which more accurately reflects his faster, more hands-and-arms-dominated swinging motion.

While you obviously want to develop a waggle (if you haven't already) that is smooth and rhythmic, rather than a series of quick, unconnected fidgets, keep in mind that you can and should actually pre-program your swing by setting it up with the type of waggle that is appropriate for the shot at hand. If you're facing a pitch from rough over a yawning bunker that you must land very softly to keep near the hole, pre-program the shot with long, slow waggling movements that include plenty of cocking action of the wrists. If you're facing a short iron shot into a strong wind and you need to punch the shot low under the gusts, your waggle should be quite different: the rhythm of the back-and-forth movements of the clubhead should be shorter and quicker, and there should not be as much break in the wrists, because you want to make a compact, firm swing that will help keep the ball low.

If you have never paid much thought to your waggle, give it some attention during your upcoming practice sessions. In particular, work on connecting your waggle to the swing itself. All of this effort in the preswing and in the waggle will help you tremendously in that it will greatly increase the consistency in the motions of the swing that follows.

SETTING IT IN MOTION: THE BACKSWING

I cannot honestly say that there is only one way to make a successful backswing. There are several world champions who have done it very differently. For example, Jack Nicklaus pushes the club straight back from

The takeaway, shown from two angles, is the foundation of the swing arc.

the ball—a slow, fairly ponderous move that includes no early wrist break. Ray Floyd, in contrast, pulls the club back quickly inside the target line with his hands, on what we'd call a "flat" backswing plane. Lee Trevino pushes the clubhead out and away from him. Fred Couples picks the club up, well outside the target line, before rerouting it later in the swing.

No one would argue that these four swings haven't worked very well. Also, let's remember that while these four champions have very different backswings, they all manage to come into the ball quite similarly and are all tremendous ball strikers. Let's also keep in mind that ball striking is only a portion of your overall performance. You can certainly become a fine player even with an unorthodox backswing. However, I think you have a better chance to become an excellent ball striker if you can develop a one-piece takeaway in which the triangle of the hands, arms, and shoulders takes the club away as one single unit.

If you look at the swings of three of my prize pupils—Greg Norman, Davis Love III, and U.S. Amateur champion Tiger Woods—you'll notice that all three players take the club back low and wide, with the clubhead appearing to be outside the hands at a point where it has moved two feet back from the ball. I prefer this type of long, low takeaway to one in which the club swings up quicker due to an early wrist cock, or one in which the clubhead swings back inside the target line, for several reasons.

Don't pick up the club too early on the backswing.

1. A low, straight-back takeaway is the foundation of a wide swing arc, which eventually translates into increased power.

2. This takeaway encourages you to shift your weight fully onto your right or rear foot on the backswing. Golfers who pick the club up too early in the backswing have a tendency to keep too much weight on the left side during the backswing. This can contribute to a swing flaw that's the bane of the amateur player, and which we'll talk about in detail later—the reverse weight shift.

3. The low, wide takeaway reduces the chances that you'll make a downswing that is too steep or choppy. You have a better chance to make a nice level clubhead movement through the ball for the most solid possible contact.

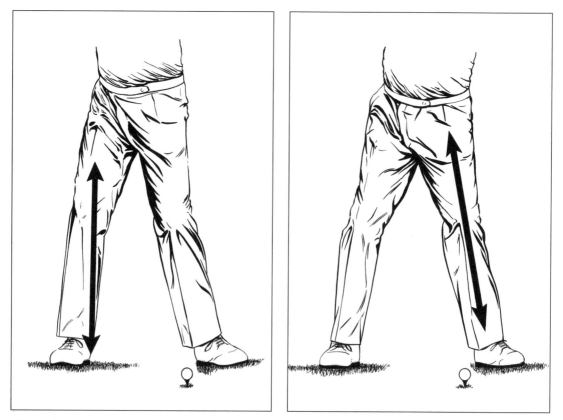

A low takeaway encourages a solid weight shift onto the right side (*left*), whereas an early wrist set causes the player to wrongly leave most of his weight on the left side during the backswing (*right*).

I believe the takeaway—the first 24 inches the clubhead moves away from the ball—should be a smooth motion, although not necessarily a slow one. The takeaway should set the pace for an even-tempoed backswing package. Don't worry about when to cock your wrists. This will begin to happen naturally when your arms have reached to about waist height and will continue through to the top-of-swing position.

As you continue back, let the swinging of the triangle trigger your hip turn. As your arms reach a certain distance to the right of your body, your weight will automatically shift onto your right foot. Let your weight go there rather than consciously turning your right hip. As you continue to swing back, simply keep in mind that you want to remain balanced on the ball of your right foot rather than getting out on your right toe. By concentrating on staying balanced on the ball of the right foot, your triangle will gradually start to pull the club along a path that's inside the target line. You don't have to do anything else to force your turn to the inside. My dad used to say, anybody who spins the right hip behind (in clockwise fashion) on the backswing, or who spins the left hip behind (counterclockwise) on the downswing, will never be a consistent winner. So move the triangle; don't spin the hips.

While striving for this shift to the right rather than a turn to the rear, remember, balance is always the key. A priority of your backswing should be to prevent your weight from ever reaching the outside of your right foot; that is, you should never actually sway to the right during the backswing. Your weight should move squarely onto your right foot without your right knee buckling outward. This was a problem Greg Norman had in his full swing up until a few years ago. At the top of Greg's old backswing his weight would get to the outside of his right foot, and his right knee would bow slightly outward. Being the superior athlete that he is, Greg got away with this flaw most of the time. However, anyone who slides laterally too far to the right on the backswing is susceptible to too much slide to the left coming back down. This motion led directly to Greg's tendency, under severe pressure, to shove or block shots to the right—a flaw that cost Greg at least one major championship and probably more. The wider stance that Greg has adopted, and which I advocate

As you swing back, maintain the flex in your right knee.

to you, has certainly helped Greg brace up his backswing shift much better than he did in the past.

In addition to adopting a fairly wide stance, make sure to keep your right knee flexed throughout the backswing. This will act as a further brace against your backswing coil and help you stay in good balance. You should feel some pressure build up on the inside of your right knee and also on the inside of your right instep and calf as the backswing pro-

The three-quarter backswing position.

gresses. This is fine. The instep of your right foot should be the main pressure point that you feel during the backswing. Just make sure to fight the pressure, to hold and contain it, rather than letting that right knee buckle outward. As you hit practice shots with this controlled weight shift in mind, you'll probably experience some fatigue in your right instep and the inside of your leg. With time, you'll get used to having this pressure, and you'll control it with less sense of strain or difficulty.

THINK "THREE QUARTERS"

All golfers want to hit the ball as far as they can—more often, they want to hit it even farther than they can. This leads to trying to make a bigger backswing than they can control. The result: a loss of control, either of the clubhead or of their own balance, with the resulting mishit shot costing them not only direction but also the distance they were hoping for in the first place. Remember, as Dad pointed out years ago before swing speed became an obsession among teachers and players—you'll hit the ball the farthest by delivering the club dead square to the back of the ball, with the clubhead moving right down the target line, the face pointing on exactly the same line as when you first lined up the club. Clubhead speed means practically nothing if the club is not delivered in this way.

Most people think of a full swing as one in which the clubshaft, at the end of the backswing, is parallel to the ground. Actually, this parallel position is really kind of an arbitrary guide to how far any individual should swing the club. A few, like John Daly, can swing the club way past parallel and still control it. For most golfers, particularly amateurs who don't play a lot and seniors who aren't as flexible as they may have been in the past, the goal of getting the club to parallel can cause problems. Often, after making a good start to the backswing as described, they'll pick the club straight up in the air with their arms, then collapse their wrists so that the club sort of flops past the parallel position. Doing this means they've lost control of both their body coil and the club. Inaccurate and weak shots are the result.

That said, when you make your backswing, think of swinging the club up to a three-quarter position. By three quarters, I mean that the clubshaft gets to a position halfway between pointing straight up and parallel with the ground. The secret to reaching this position, consistently, is turning the shoulders fully, restricting hip turn, and not letting your hands and arms swing back as far as is physically possible.

Greg Norman proves you don't have to swing past parallel, like John Daly, to generate power.

As confirmation that you can achieve plenty of distance with a swing that does not reach parallel, look at Greg Norman at the top of his backswing. As opposed to Greg's 1980s swing, in which the driver clubhead reached past parallel, presently Norman's clubshaft, at the top of his backswing, is at the three-quarter position. Yet Greg, even at age 40, booms it as long as ever. In 1994, he ranked eighth on the Tour in driving distance at 277.1 yards.

Whatever amount of controlled turn you can make while feeling as if you have something in reserve is the right length of backswing for you. We'll talk more about

For most right-handed players, one question that often arises is, "How much should I lift my left heel on the backswing?" I always get a kick when my students ask this question, because they assume that a golfer is supposed to lift up the left heel as a conscious movement in the swing.

Let me make this clear right now: The left heel, if it raises near the top of the backswing, does so only as a chain-reaction response to the coil of the upper body, which in turn pulls the hip upward, which exerts an upward pull on the lower left leg and foot. In other words, if it moves off the ground, the left heel is the last thing to move. You should never consciously lift the left heel.

The more supple you are, the less likely it will be that your left heel gets pulled up. Of course, the more backswing coil you are trying to produce, the more likely it is that your left heel will rise. So, it's more likely that you will get some left heel lift on your tee shots, where you're striving for good distance, than on your shorter iron shots. But bearing in mind the concept of keeping your swing length at 75 percent of your maximum, I like to see the left heel lift only slightly or, better yet, stay on the ground with just a slight turning of the weight onto the inside of the heel. This is in keeping with the theory that the fewer moving parts there are to the swing, the better.

this when it's time to discuss physical conditioning. My feeling is that you can increase the length of your backswing by increasing your suppleness and strength. Don't try to make a long backswing that is not a controlled backswing.

SWING WITH DRIVER VS. IRONS

While most of the elements that make up a good golf swing are the same for any club, there are some slight variations between the driver swing and the iron swing, so let's take a moment to discuss them.

The most effective driver swing is one that delivers the clubhead to the ball on a level or sweeping swing plane. The reason for this is that you can't hit down on the ball with a club that has between one and eleven degrees of loft and obtain the optimum carry and roll. The driver must meet the ball on a level plain.

For the club to be moving through impact at a shallow angle, the entire swing must be on a relatively shallow plane, a little more around the body than up and down. A good way to accomplish this is, after the initial takeaway move of your triangle, to continue the backswing by swinging your left forearm more across your chest than upward. I don't agree with teachers who tell students to reach for the sky on the backswing. This creates separation of the arms from the body rather than having the body and arms swing as a unit. And it definitely creates too steep an angle of attack on the downswing, particularly for the driver. I might add that Greg Norman, whose swing was quite upright in the 1980s, has flattened his swing plane with the driver considerably in the last few years and has gained great accuracy to go with his distance.

With the irons, particularly the shorter irons, it's okay to be slightly more upright, so that the clubhead meets the ball with a slightly descending blow, to give the shot backspin and a soft landing. But notice that I said slightly descending. You never want to make a swing in which the club drives down on the ball and gouges out a deep divot, resulting in a "fat" shot. A moderately shallow angle of attack, even with the pitching clubs, will give your shotmaking the greatest consistency.

HEAD POSITION

Let's talk now about that one teaching tenet that even every beginner knows about—but one that can actually cause you some problems if not understood completely. This is the advice to keep your head still. Many amateurs are so preoccupied with keeping their head still that they don't make much of a backswing coil at all.

As you shift your weight onto your right side and move the triangle back, I believe it's not only okay, but necessary, to allow your head to shift slightly back to the right, away from your target. In my opinion, a level movement of the head of two to three inches away from the target is acceptable, particularly with the driver. However, there should never be any vertical, up-and-down movement of the head during any part of the swing until well into the follow-through. Vertical movement of the head and/or upper body can only cause those frustrating bad shots—either fat or topped.

DOWNSWING: SLIDE, THEN TURN

The best downswing move starts from the ground up. If your left heel rises at the top of the backswing, your first move should be to replant it firmly, thereby moving most of your weight solidly onto your left side. If your left heel remains grounded at the top, your downswing key is to slide your left hip laterally toward the target.

My dad considered Ben Hogan to have the best downswing hip action of all time. He had a film of Mr. Hogan that proved this technical point. Funnily enough, Mr. Hogan's hip slide during the downswing was highlighted by the fact that, in the film, there was a man on the bench behind him who appeared just to the left of Ben's left hip. At the top of Ben's backswing you could see this guy, but at impact, his left hip had moved so far laterally that the guy was blocked out of the picture.

The start-down position.

From the top of the backswing, your left hip should slide between 6 and 12 inches laterally toward the target during the downswing. Note that this does not mean the hips should be 6 to 12 inches ahead of where they were at the start of the swing. It means they should slide that distance laterally from where they had shifted back to at the top of the backswing. Once your hips have completed their slide, they should then rotate behind you in a counterclockwise fashion. Just remember that you should never consciously spin the hip behind you, with no lateral slide, on either the backswing or the downswing.

The best ball strikers have all had great hip action. Of course I am prejudiced, but in the 1940s and 1950s, I believe that the two finest strikers of the ball were Ben

Greg Norman's fluid hip action promotes power.

Hogan and my dad. Today, I would go with Greg Norman and Nick Faldo. All of these players had or have great hip action through the downswing.

One point that I think a lot of amateurs get confused about is that they try to drive their legs at the target rather than make a lateral hip slide. The two are not the same.

The left hip (for the right-handed player) should be the part of the body that is closest to the target early in the downswing. When a person tries to drive with the legs, their bowed left knee gets well out in front of its original position at address. This can cause you to lose balance and mishit shots in general. You'll also get too far in front of the ball so that you can't return the clubface to a square position at impact, resulting in shots pushed to the right.

TAKE IT FROM THE TOP

The most natural thing for most golfers to do at the top of the backswing is to start the club back down with their hands. This is also one of the most destructive things you can do to a golf swing.

Even though it might go against your natural inclinations, you must learn to make the first move down with your lower left side. Here's a good practice drill that will help you get the feel of the lateral slide of the left hip toward the target in order to start the downswing. Bring the clubhead up to your normal top-of-the-backswing position and stop. After pausing for two to three seconds, swing back down, making sure that your lower body leads the action. It's much easier to feel the correct move when you start the downswing from a fixed position than it is when the club is swung up to the top without a pause. And by learning to start down with the lower body, you automatically eliminate another harmful move; "throwing" the right shoulder (and with it the clubhead) to the outside in relation to your target line. When you make a good lower body move, the very fact that your hands, right arm, and shoulder remain passive means that they will stay tucked in close to the body as the downswing commences—right where they belong.

I offered this suggestion to Fred Couples at the 1995 Tournament of Champions, and he felt the drill helped him time his downswing better. In fact, he won the next two tournaments he played in.

Swinging into impact.

If you've played golf for a while, you are probably familiar with the term *release the clubhead*. It is usually discussed in the context of making the hands manipulate the clubface so that it moves from a relatively open position in relation to the target line prior to impact, to a square position as clubhead meets ball. Unfortunately, very few golfers have the quickness and high degree of hand-eye coordination that it would take to time the release by closing the clubface with their hands at just the right instant.

You may also have heard the argument that if you've done everything right leading up to the instant when the club flashes through the impact zone, you should not have to worry about releasing the club at all. Frankly, I wish it were true that everyone automatically releases the club with no conscious effort. But just to drive home the point that this is not the case, let me ask you a hypothetical question.

Suppose you sat beside a tee of a long par-four hole at any course in America, a hole where most every player used a driver, and you counted how many tee shots started right of the target. Do you think only, say, one third of all shots would be in this category? My guess is that over 80 percent of all shots by amateurs miss the target, often substantially, with the ball starting to the right. This means that the clubface was not squared up to the target in time for impact.

So, I contend that there must be a conscious effort to square the clubface—by most players. However, I've already stated that trying to do so with your hands is nearly impossible. So, here's a suggestion that I've found most people can visualize and implement to help them square the clubface at impact. It's simply this: After you've started the downswing with your lower-body lead, and your hands and arms have reached a position opposite your right hip, think in terms of rotating your right forearm over your left through the impact zone. You can do this with your arms in a smooth, rhythmic motion as opposed to a sense of flipping the club with your hands, which more often than not will lead to a disastrous result. It's not a difficult movement to implement, and will definitely help you if you're suffering from a case of the "right to rights."

FOLLOWING THROUGH

Past impact, if you have done everything as described and, particularly, have made your downswing move from the ground up, the momentum you will have built through impact will be so strong that the follow-through should almost take care of itself. However, many amateurs have an incorrect notion of what should happen after impact.

The momentum of the downswing should carry the club around the body, but most amateurs seem to think that they should swing the club around and up. Past impact, they add a conscious lifting motion with their arms and body that is not only unnecessary but harmful.

Past impact, your right forearm should be crossing over your left, as we've discussed. Meanwhile, the clubhead will be flashing rapidly to the left of the target line as the follow-through continues. Many amateurs believe that they must keep the clubhead on the target line after impact. This thought only leads to a blocking action through impact, and is the cause of so many shots that are hit well right of the target.

Let your body keep rotating freely in a counterclockwise fashion, and let the club swing in the same direction. You should finish with 90 percent of your weight on your left foot, while also being nicely balanced on your right toe.

The follow-through (*left*).The finish (*right*).

The Simple Yet Endlessly Complex Short Game

As we touched on earlier, the average golfer plays as many shots from within 75 yards of the hole as from outside 75 yards—and this does not even count all the "gimme" putts during a round. If you truly want to maximize your score, you must treat the short game with the respect it deserves.

I think you'll find it enlightening, if you ever have the chance, to attend a pro Tour event, particularly on Tuesday, which is the main practice day for players, since the course is usually tied up by a pro-am on Wednesdays. Watch the best players in the world practice. Assuming they are not holding anyone else up, they will test as many little shots as they can around the greens as they move around the course. They take note of likely spots where the ball will land if they miss the green— observing the grass in that particular area and the resistance it gives to the clubhead, testing the consistency of the sand in the bunkers, noting if the edges of the greens where chip shots might land are firm or soft, gauging the consistency of the fringes so they'll know if they can putt rather than chip from them. Watch how many players work on the practice green or the chipping/sand-play areas. I think you'll be really surprised by what you see, but then it will dawn on you: these players are so great around the greens because practicing the short game is almost a religion to them.

Whether you practice on the course or hit a variety of shots in a backyard short-game area, as Greg Norman does, you must realize that in

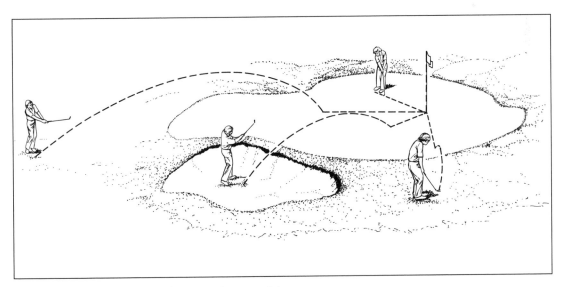

Pitching, sand play, chipping, and putting: the guts of the game.

order to score, sometimes hitting drives has to take a back seat to working with the wedges.

When my dad had the practice green at Winged Foot Golf Club available to him in the early evening, he would arrange the best possible short-game practice. He'd take a shag bag with about a hundred balls and, starting perhaps 75 yards from the pin, he'd scatter them, drop them anywhere off the green, and then play them all to the pin. He'd face pitches from all kinds of rough, lobs over bunkers, long-running chips, short chips from rough, short chips from fringe, short bunker shots, long bunker shots—you name it, he'd play it. No wonder Dad was one of the best of his time in this area of the game.

Whenever you practice the short game, hone in on that target. Play each of your shots as if you needed to get it up and down to win your club championship, or whatever event it is that you hope to win. Better still, practice with your friends. Invent contests, for example, to see who can get "up and down" the most times on ten different short-game shots. Put a small wager on the outcome, such as lunch or a sleeve of golf balls. You need to put a little pressure on yourself, and maybe a little more on the short game than on the full shots. It's amazing how many amateurs, when they need to play a delicate chip well or need a straight-in three-footer to halve the match, will suddenly fluff the shot even if they've been playing it well most of the day.

If you put some pressure on your short game through intelligent and focused practice, believe me, you'll be much more confident when you run into those touchy short-game situations during actual competition.

A BASIC APPROACH TO CHIPPING

I believe there is one basic tenet that will help every golfer in the area of chipping: Make the ball carry as little as possible and roll as far as possible to the cup.

Of course, if you were to take this advice to the extreme, it would mean that you would not use any lofted clubs in chipping, but rather would putt the ball from off the green every time. This is not realistic, because in most cases, you will be far enough off the green and/or in a rough or fringe area in which the ball would get "snuffed" if rolled with the putter. So, the most realistic approach is to chip with a club that has enough loft so that it lands the ball safely onto the green, with enough

To promote a running chip, play the ball back in your stance.

momentum to let the ball run to the hole. You always want the ball to land on the putting surface so that it gets the truest possible bounce and roll from there.

Next, let's build a little bit of a cushion into your assessment of the shot to make sure you get the ball on the green for a true roll. Suppose you are 6 feet off the green, and a 6-iron would be the club that would carry the ball 6 or 7 feet so that it would just land on the green and then run the correct distance to the hole. In this case, I would tell you that the correct club would be, not the 6-iron, but instead a 7-iron. You want to give yourself a little cushion in landing the ball on the green, so take a club that will land the ball, say, 4 or 5 feet onto the surface instead of just a foot or so, while still having the right amount of momentum to stop at the flag. Then, if you hit your chip shot a tiny bit thin, the ball will still land on the green and take that true first bounce.

DON'T BE TOO FORMULA-ORIENTED

If you have read any other books or magazine articles on chipping, you may have come across attempts to develop a formula with which to select the right club for any given chip. For example, a 7-iron gives one quarter of the distance in carry, three fourths in roll; a pitching wedge, one-half carry and one-half roll; and so on. In general, these formulas are usually not too far off the mark, but to become a polished short-game player, you really need to play with a greater sense of feel than that!

You see, all of the greens, and the chipping areas surrounding them, are sort of like human faces, with individual features and contours that are theirs and theirs alone. Aside from the total length of any given chip, the shot can be flat, uphill, or downhill along its entire length. Or it can be flat for a while, then work uphill near the hole, or vice versa. It can break left, break right. It can be played to a green that is slow, medium or lightning fast. Your chip can land on an area where the green is soft, although the green nearer the hole may be harder. You may be chipping off a nice, short, tight piece of turf, so the ball will take a little backspin, or you may be chipping from some tufted rough which may make the ball run a little more than usual. All of these factors are going to have some

One difference between the chipping game of the Tour pro and that of the average amateur is that the pro will leave the ball in a position (if it is not actually within "gimme" range) from which a one-putt is relatively simple. The amateur thinks more generally about hitting the ball close, often leaving trickier putts to deal with.

Let's put the ball in a position on the front-right fringe of a green that slopes fairly sharply from back to front, with the pin on the left-middle of the sloping green. The pro knows that, if anything, a straight uphill putt is the desired one (next to holing the chip and having no putt at all), so he'll make sure that he leaves the ball on the "low" side of the hole, say 4 feet to the left of it.

The amateur, meanwhile, doesn't think this far ahead. He or she just generally tries to make a good chip, and in doing so runs it a bit past the cup on the "high" side. While everyone's thinking that was a great shot, what the player is left with is a touchy downhill, left-to-right breaking slider. The pro, who left the ball below the hole, has an excellent chance to complete the "up and down," while the amateur may at best have a 50–50 chance with that much tougher putt. So, plan ahead to leave yourself the simplest remaining putt.

effect on the amount of carry and roll you should plan into the shot and, therefore, which club you should choose.

You just can't boil your chipping game down to a formula. Instead, practice your chipping from different lies, from different angles to different pin positions. Get a feel for the clubs that give you the best results. Depending on the situation, you might be able to chip with anything from, say, a 2-iron all the way to a lob wedge.

PLAY THE "SAFE STROKE"

The chipping stroke itself is really quite simple. There's no need to show you any complicated techniques. For all basic chips, your goal is simply to strike the ball with a nice little descending blow, making sure that you contact the ball first, then nip the grass just slightly after making contact. Your main goal is to always contact the ball before the turf. As I touched on earlier, if the club contacts the ball a little low on the face, the ball may fly a little lower than you expected, but it will usually run a little farther, so that the overall result of the shot will be the same. If, however, you catch a little turf before the ball—that is, hit the chip "fat"—then you are guaranteed to lose some of the energy needed to get the ball to the hole. (If you hit it really fat, you then have the classic "chili dip," in which the ball doesn't even get to the green.)

Keeping this in mind, you'll want to set up to the ball so that you virtually eliminate the chances of hitting the ball fat. Assume a narrow, slightly open stance in which your weight is leaning decidedly on your left foot. Position the ball near the inside of your right foot, while your hands are positioned well ahead of the ball, opposite the crease in your left pants leg. This sets you up for the desired downward angle of attack of the clubhead onto the ball. A good checkpoint for your hand position is to make sure that your right wrist is bent back at a slight angle, rather than flat. Another way to confirm that your hand position is correct is to let go of the club; the handle should rest on your left thigh.

Whether one chips with a sand wedge (*above*), a favorite 7-iron, or any other club, a good chipper positions his hands ahead of the ball.

As to the stroke itself, it is basically a one-piece movement with the hands and arms working as a unit. Take the club straight back from the ball, your hands and wrists staying relatively firm. The length of the stroke is something you can determine only through constant practice of varying chip shots. The shorter the chip, the firmer your hands and wrists will stay throughout the stroke. Say, for example, you are chipping from the fringe to a cup that's only 25

When chipping, make a one-piece takeaway action.

feet away, and the green is fairly fast. For this chip, your stroke will be so short that it will be just like a putt, with almost no wrist movement. However, let's consider another situation, where you have a wedge chip from light rough, the pin is 75 feet away, and the green is slower. Here, you'll do everything the same, but your swing will be longer because you must generate more carry and roll. For this longer chip, I do not recommend that you force your wrists to be rigid throughout the stroke. Simply feel how much swing you need for the distance. Your takeaway will be firm, but allow the wrists to cock ever so slightly at the top of the stroke to encourage feel for the clubhead.

Make sure to pull the club back through the ball with the hands leading the clubface down and through. Consistently clean contact will mean that the ball will react as you visualized it. If you made the right read and picked the right club for the job, the result may be that you're close enough that you don't even need to putt it.

THE PITCHING GAME: A FIRM APPROACH IS BEST

Let's move off the green a bit and cross that boundary after which chip shots turn into pitch shots. The demarcation point is a little hard to define and is somewhat a matter of opinion. But for our purposes, let's define pitch shots as:

1. Shots that are played with one of the wedges—pitching, approach, sand, or lob.
2. Shots that also must carry a minimum of 20 yards in the air. Anything shorter than this could be considered a chip, not a pitch.

In point number 1 above, I mentioned four different wedges. This may be a little surprising to you in that most commonly golfers carry two wedges, pitching and sand. We've seen how many chips and pitches the average amateur plays; I think that most readers will benefit from adding at least one more wedge to their bag—either an "approach" wedge or a "lob" wedge.

In contemporary club design, there is often quite a difference between the lofts of the pitching wedge (often around 47 degrees) and the sand wedge (usually around 55 degrees). This is an 8-degree difference, while the difference in loft among all the other clubs is usually no more than 4 degrees (and sometimes less). For example, a 2-iron features 20 degrees of loft, a 3-iron 24 degrees.

An "approach" or "gap" wedge fits between the pitching and sand wedges, with somewhere in the vicinity of 51 degrees loft. It can come in very handy both on certain short pitches around the green and, of course, on longer shots that are out of range with your sand wedge, but which you would have to ease up on with your pitching wedge, particularly if it has 47 or fewer degrees of loft.

The "lob" wedge, meanwhile, has more loft than even the sand wedge, usually around 60 degrees. It is a blessing whenever you have to play a high, soft pitch from rough and have little green to work with. In addition, the lob wedge is designed differently from the sand wedge in that it has a less protruding flange (which is needed to make the sand wedge "bounce" in sand, as we'll see shortly). This means the club is even easier to play than the sand wedge from different fairway lies.

I recommend that you check the playing characteristics of your pitching and sand wedges, particularly these clubs' lofts; and also, think about the demands of your course in terms of short-game shots. If your greens are fast and have a good deal of contour, and if the course is demanding in terms of rough and slopes around the greens, I recommend that you add at least one wedge to your pitching arsenal.

That said, let's move on to the execution of the pitch shot.

KEEP IT SIMPLE, NOT "SPINFUL"

There are an endless number of variations on the pitching swing, each of which depends on the particulars of the shot situation that you face, particularly the lie of the ball. You could write a book solely about playing all the different pitch shots, believe me. Time and space do not permit this here, but I would at least like to explain the basic pitch swing. It's up to you to practice all the variations and to develop an innate feel for each of them.

The pitch swing does not vary much from the swing you will make with your middle and short irons. At address, maintain a fairly wide stance, with the inside of your heels a good 8 to 10 inches apart. You may wish to put a little more than half your weight on your left or forward foot, but for the sake of good balance, never stray too much from that 50/50 weight distribution.

The setup used for pitching.

Your body alignment should be a shade open, pointing a little left of "parallel left" for the right-handed golfer. This adjustment will allow you to put a trace of out-to-in cut spin on your pitch shots, which is usually helpful since this helps the ball up out of poorer lies and also helps it come to a quick stop.

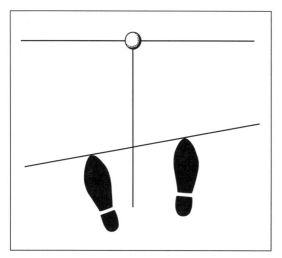

When setting up to hit a full pitch shot, assume a slightly "open" stance by placing your right foot closer to the imaginary ball-target line.

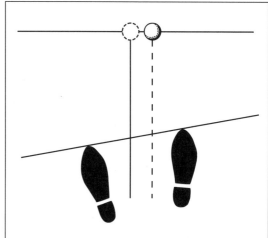

To play a specialty shot, such as the pitch-and-run, move the ball back in your stance.

Position the ball approximately in the middle of your stance for the basic full pitch shot, or maybe a ball width ahead of center. One flaw I see with a lot of amateurs, and even some pros, is that they play the ball too far back in the stance and try to hit down too sharply. For most players, this will lead to poor results in the form of a lot of fat shots. Play the ball back of center in your stance only if you wish to play a low pitch-and-run shot, which is useful when the pin is located at the back of a long green. Play the ball off the forward foot only when looking for added height.

If you observe the great pitchers of the ball—players like Curtis Strange, Tom Kite, and Corey Pavin—you'll notice that they never hit a pitch shot all out. Instead, they use a three-quarter-length swing. You should follow their example. There is no need whatsoever to overpower a pitch shot. This shot is really all about precise delivery of the clubhead through the ball. If you think a certain pitch is just out of your range with a sand iron and a three-quarter swing, use a pitching wedge (or your "approach" wedge, if you carry one).

There will also be many shots with the pitching clubs that require *less* than a three-quarter swing, since, as we noted, pitch shots can have as short a carry as 20 yards. Developing the right feel for distance and the amount of swing needed with any of the wedges for any given shot is, of course, something you must learn by practicing all types of pitch shots.

In making this three-quarter backswing, again swing the triangle of your hands, arms, and shoulders back in one piece, for a fairly low, controlled takeaway. As you swing back, make sure to keep the inside of your right leg braced against your weight shift to the right. Try to keep your wrists firm all the way to the top of your three-quarter position. I have seen more wedge shots missed because of loose wrist action than for any

The pitch shot does not require a big backswing.   Play the ball "up" to promote extra height.

other reason. Unless you are in certain types of unusually difficult lies, there is no need to be wristy on these shots.

Another trait of good wedge players is that they nip the ball just before the bottom of their downswing. They take just a slight divot, if any, after impact. So, once you've reached the top, don't make a hard downswing move onto your left side, but rather a smooth, balanced one, so that your body weight is in about the same position that it was at address and your head has not moved ahead of the ball. This will give you a shot that utilizes the true loft of the club, and shots that, given a reasonably good lie, will land softly and stop quietly after just one small hop.

NEVER "SCOOP" THE BALL

While some golfers try to hit down too hard on their pitch shots, probably even more golfers try to help their pitch shots into the air with an independent, scooping action of the hands and wrists. This is an even bigger fault than hitting down too steeply. Again, the most likely result is catching the ground first and hitting the ball fat, but this move is also a common cause of catching the ball in its middle while the club is on the upswing, resulting in a skulled shot. There is no need to help this shot up with any independent scooping actions. Trust the loft on your wedges.

In cases where you need to hit the ball extra high, it's okay to move the ball a little forward in your stance, perhaps two to three inches ahead of center. Then go ahead and use your normal pitching swing. A word of warning, though: Make sure your lie gives you a fair amount of cushion under the ball whenever you are trying to hit an extra-high pitch shot. You'll actually find it easiest to play the high pitch out of good lies in light rough.

Here's a good drill to get the feel of the correct arm action through impact to pitch the ball high or low: Stand facing a target about 30 feet away, with a ball in your right hand (if you're a right-handed player). For the feel of a high shot, throw the ball underhanded high in the air, and try to make it land near the target. For the lower pitch, again hold the ball in your right hand, then swing your arm toward the target, releasing the ball much earlier so that the ball flies toward the target on the trajectory of a softball pitch. The in-flight trajectory of each throw will simulate a well-played pitch shot.

PUTTING: THE GAME WITHIN A GAME

The putting stroke is probably the game's most individualistic area. In keeping with my theory that you don't teach golfers a single way to play, but rather you teach them how to play golf, I believe that when it comes to putting, you do what you feel confident with in regard to your setup and grip, your stroke, and the putter you choose.

There are a remarkable number of great putters whose styles are completely different from one another. Many players are now going to the cross-handed putting style, some are having success with various long putters, and some are even putting one-handed! However, I still recommend what's known as the reverse overlap grip. This grip is one in

Putting: that "other" game.

which, instead of overlapping your right little finger over your left index finger, you overlap your left index finger over your right forefinger or the fingers of your right hand. The benefit of this grip is that it keeps all five fingers of the right hand on the grip; for most people, this creates an optimum feel for distance.

Keeping in mind the ever-widening number of putting setups and grips that are being used successfully, I would like to encourage you to remember just two key things while developing your own personal style of putting.

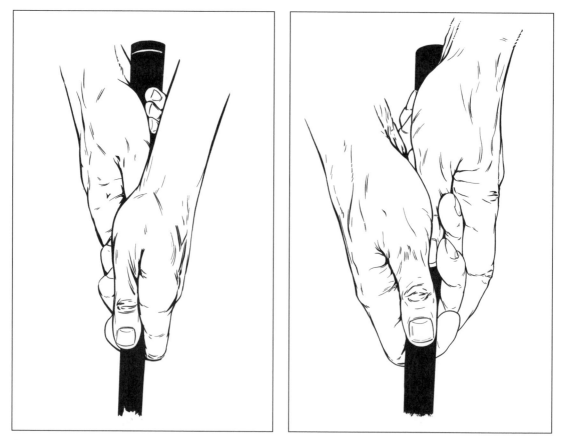

Although the cross-handed putting grip (*left*) is "hot," the reverse overlap grip (*right*) is still the most popular hold among pro and amateur players.

1. When preparing to putt, set your blade down as squarely as possible to the line you've chosen, then build a setup that is comfortable and secure around that square blade.

2. Always strive to keep your head perfectly still throughout the stroke—preferably until you've heard the ball plunk into the cup. The putt is entirely different from any other golf stroke in that there is virtually no need to develop power through the shifting of any body weight. Putting is entirely a matter of precision. Keeping your head steady is the best thing you can do to guarantee that you will return the putter blade at impact to precisely where you started it.

While your posture and body alignment are very personal in putting, the key element to successful putting is making sure that your putterhead is perfectly aligned to the correct starting line of the putt. Alignment can be a little more complex in putting than in hitting full shots, where you know exactly where you want to aim. On the greens, you must make your read of the putt, and then determine, very precisely, the line on which the ball must start in order to take the break, if any, into the cup. And you must make sure to direct the putter to that starting line only. It's very easy on breaking putts, as you're getting set over the ball, to unconsciously align the putter more toward the cup itself and slightly away from that critical starting line. Make sure to set the putter on your starting line and be aware that it must stay there.

As to the stroke itself, you may have heard from some teachers that the putterhead should be kept square to the target, and moving directly along your chosen line of putt throughout the entire stroke. I don't agree with this. While in theory it sounds like a good idea, in actuality it tends to make for an unnatural, "wooden," or stiff, stroke.

I think you'll get the best results on the green if you swing the putter with the triangle of your hands, arms, and shoulders, as Greg Norman and many other good modern-day putters do. When you do this, as with your full shots, the clubhead will gradually swing inside the target line on the backstroke, come back to meet the target line (and the ball) and then gradually swing back to the inside of the target line past impact. This

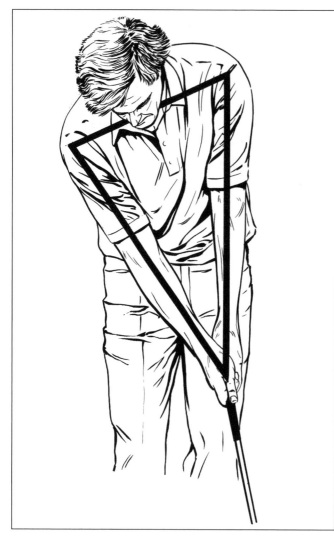

Like most good putters, Greg Norman swings the club by moving the triangle formed by his arms and shoulders.

"inside-to-inside" movement is almost imperceptible on putts of under six feet. The longer the putt and the stroke, though, the more the clubhead will swing inside the target line.

Keep in mind that there is no unnatural manipulation of the clubhead at all during this stroke. The hands do not move the putterface in any way. Furthermore, while the putterhead swings to the inside, the putterface remains square to the *path* of the stroke itself. If the putterhead remains square to the path throughout the entire stroke, this means it will automatically be square to the *target* line at impact. You should not try to keep the putterface pointed directly at the target throughout the entire stroke, because to do so you would have to manipulate the putterface with your hands and forearms in an unnatural way.

How far do you swing the putter for any given length of putt? That's putting's $64,000 question. Unfortunately, it's unanswerable. That's because, as in chipping, every putt is a little bit different, a little more either uphill, downhill, or sidehill, over longer or shorter or hardier or thinner grass, over a surface that's damp or one that's dry. There's no substitute for constant prac-

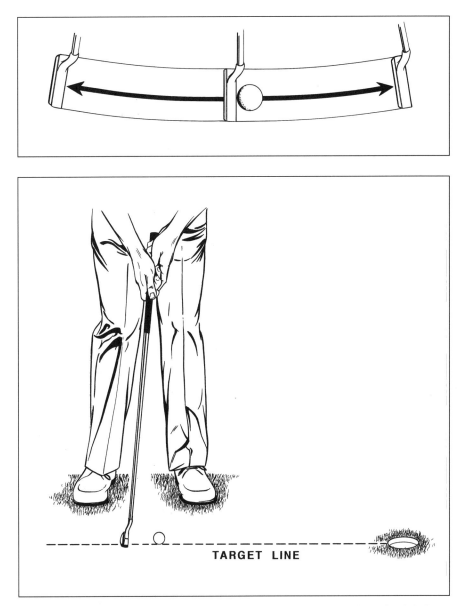

TARGET LINE

Good putters let the putter swing on an inside-square-inside path (*above*), while less-talented putters use their hands to manipulate the stroke (*below*). Trying to force the putterface to stay square to the hole makes you grip the putter extrafirmly; in turn, this grip creates tension in the arms, thereby hindering your feel and distance control.

tice. You have to develop a feel for putting, with awareness. Distance is a more critical factor in putting than direction; if you can learn to hit putts from all distances, over all surfaces, with confidence that you can keep your speed so that the ball stops within a two-foot radius of the hole, you'll rarely three-putt.

Here's a drill that I think will help you tremendously in learning to control distance and cure the "yips." On the practice green, drop some balls at various distances and angles, from 20 to 35 feet from the hole. Read the putt and set up to the line as you normally would; then, before you execute the stroke, close your eyes—and then stroke the putt. Don't open your eyes until after you have determined from the feel of impact whether the putt's distance is short, long, or just right. When you get to the point where you can predict your distance on every putt, believe me, you've made great strides toward becoming an excellent putter.

STICK WITH THE PUTTER YOU LOVE

If you've played a lot of golf, you've probably heard many theories about putters and possibly tried a lot of different models. There are all types of blade, flanged-blade, heel-toe-weighted, and mallet-style putters available, and most all of them can do the job for someone. I think some experimenting is good, but I don't believe you should change putters because a certain style is hot or because your favorite Tour pro is now using it.

Neither do I think you should change putters for different types of greens. In other words, don't try to find a heavy putter to use on greens that are slow, and a light one for when you're on quick surfaces. Instead, find the one whose clubhead style strikes your eye just right, and also one whose lie fits your setup style, with the sole lying flat against the surface. Most people don't realize this, but when a putter's lie is incorrect, its face will misalign slightly too.

One area of putter design you need to know about, and again most amateurs don't, is the club's loft. Almost every putter has some loft to it, to get the ball rolling above the grass surface rather than pushing the ball

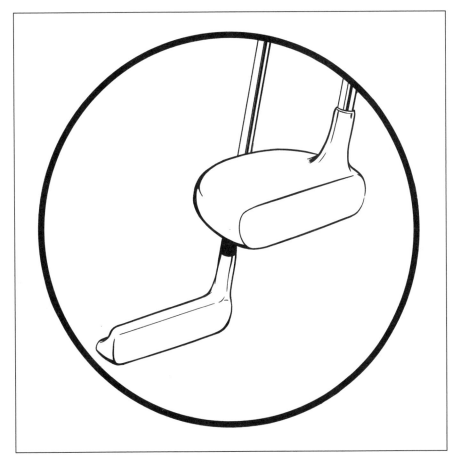

Two popular putter types: the flanged blade (*left*); the mallet (*above, right*).

downward. This loft can range from about 2 to 8 degrees. Unless you putt on greens that are extremely smooth, I recommend you use a putter with a little more loft, say 6 to 7 degrees, as opposed to a very low-lofted putter. But remember, once you've found the putter you like, stick with it throughout your game.

To add distance control to your stroke, work on this drill:

Address a short putt (4 to 8 feet) normally, then take your left hand off the handle and place it by your left pants pocket. Stroke putts with your right hand only, swinging the club back low to the ground and then through to the target. Try to accelerate the putter on the down-stroke and hit the putt as solidly as you can. You may find that your control of the club is a little shaky at first, but keep working on it. When you get on the course with both hands on the grip, you'll feel as though delivering the clubface perfectly along your target line will be a snap.

Putting one-handed can help you learn how to better judge distance.

Here's a fun way to groove your stroke and, at the same time, gain immediate feedback as to any errors in your delivery of the clubface at impact. Drop a few balls on the practice green, 8 feet from the hole. Then, midway between you and the hole, set up two tees that will act as goalposts, on either side of the perfect line to the cup. These goalposts should be set only about as wide as the blade of your putter from toe to heel—about 4 inches apart. Simply try to roll your putts between the goalposts. If you hit the left tee, you immediately know your clubface was closed in relation to the target line or that your path was to the left of your tar-

get. If the ball contacts the tee on the right, you know you've left the clubface open or that your path was to the right. Keep working on your alignment and your stroke until you can roll ten field goals in a row between the "uprights." If you get the ball through the uprights untouched, you'll make almost all of these 8-foot putts.

The "field goal" drill will help you detect faults in your stroke.

I'd like to describe a widely misunderstood method of reading the line of a putt. This is the method known as "plumb-bobbing."

First, the correct method: Stand or squat behind your ball, with your dominant eye directly on a line with the hole and your ball. Raise your puttershaft in front of your eye, holding it between your fingers near the top of the grip so that it hangs straight down. The puttershaft should bisect the hole.

The "plumb-bob" method for determining how the green slopes.

Here's where the misconception about plumb-bobbing comes in. Many people believe that using the clubshaft as a plumb-bob device is supposed to tell them how much the putt is going to break. In other words, I've seen it described that as you line up the putter with your dominant eye, the shaft should be to one side or the other of the hole, and the number of inches that the shaft lies to one side or the other of the hole is the amount that the putt is going to break.

Well, let me clear something up right here. The only reason the shaft appears to be on one side of the hole or the other is that the player has not lined up the shaft, ball, and cup correctly. There is no way that plumb-bobbing visually shows you how much a putt is going to break.

What plumb-bobbing will show you, if done correctly, is this. As you line up the putter-shaft over the ball and the hole, you get a split view of the terrain on either side of the cup. This will help you see how much the ground slopes in one direction or the other, in relation to a perfect vertical line, which is your clubshaft. The more slope you see in relation to this vertical line, let's say, to the right, the more break to the right you can predict in the putt. But plumb-bobbing itself does not tell you exactly how many inches of break to play for.

Plumb-bobbing is useful in that it can clarify for you which way the terrain slopes— if it slopes at all. It will be more helpful to you on putts with small, hard-to-see breaks than on severe slopes, which you will be able to notice without the aid of a vertical plumb-bob.

Greg Norman and Ben Crenshaw are two players who revert to the plumb-bob method if they are baffled after reading the line from behind the ball.

Before plumb-bobbing, try to figure the break from behind the ball, as Greg Norman does.

Almost all golfers who have played for a long time have run into periods when they have totally lost confidence in their stroke. When it gets to the point where the player has gotten so nervous that he or she can no longer put a normal smooth stroke on the ball, unfortunately, it's become a case of the yips.

While I hope this doesn't happen to you, if you get to the point where your stroke has become nervous and jerky, I recommend the following prescription, to be used either on the practice green or, yes, on the golf course itself.

Simply do this: Line up your putt and set up to the ball as you normally do, looking back and forth from ball to hole until you have the feel for distance and the force of stroke needed. When you look down at the ball for the last time, close your eyes, then make your normal stroke. Closing your eyes will help you to bypass the panicky feeling you get while looking at the ball and tightening up just prior to starting the stroke. Simply relax, close your eyes, trust your stroke, and go.

This tip may sound a bit outrageous, especially if you are really shook up about your stroke at the moment. Please trust me and, as they say on the sports commercials, "Just do it." I'll bet you can get back to making your smoothest, best stroke if you do it with your eyes closed. Keep using this method and gradually your fear of the putts will fade away, and before you know it you'll have your smooth stroke back.

OUT OF THE SAND WITH ONE HAND

Let's spend a few minutes on the final segment of short-game play, the one at which so many amateurs are needlessly deficient: sand play. What I will tell you here is basically coming straight from one of the true masters of sand play, my dad. What you read here may be a little different from what you may have heard before, but believe me, Dad's system works.

There are three key elements to understand in order to immediately improve your sand play.

1. For a right-handed player, the sand shot is executed almost entirely by the right hand slapping or thumping the sand behind the ball.

2. The distance you should strike the sand behind the ball with this right-handed thump is much farther than most golfers realize—at least 3 inches behind the ball.

3. You will make the sand shot much, much easier if you have a good sand wedge—one that has a large flange and a high degree of "bounce" built into the sole. (Bounce means the degree to which the back or rear edge of the flange lies below the leading edge of the flange, when the clubshaft is held in a vertical position.)

To execute the basic sand shot, grip the club with your left hand (left thumb on top of the shaft) and your right hand a little lower down

The sand shot.

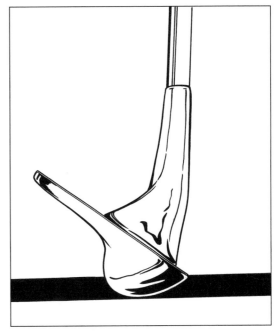

When choosing a sand wedge, pick one with a good degree of bounce.

On sand shots, an open stance and open clubface position are two critical setup keys—as Claude Harmon, Sr. demonstrates.

In playing the basic sand shot, swing the club sharply upward with your right hand.

the handle than normal. This will counterbalance the fact that you'll be a little closer to the ball after wiggling your feet into a secure stance in the sand. Then, open the face of your sand wedge wide, so that it's aimed quite a bit right of your target.

Next, open your stance so that your body aligns well to the left of the flag. Understand that this will bring your clubface back close to square; that is, it is now aiming only a little to the right of the target. Keep the majority of your weight on your left side.

Position the ball well forward in relation to your opened stance. Because the stance is so open, to the observer who is looking from directly opposite you and perpendicular to your target line, it will look as though the ball is positioned well in front of your left toe. However, the leading edge of your sand iron should be about 3 inches behind the ball.

The swing itself should be controlled completely with your right hand—your left is merely going along for a ride. Keeping your weight on your left side, swing the club sharply upward with your right hand, cocking the wrist much earlier than you would for your normal fairway shots. At the top, you'll want the left wrist to be in a cupped position.

As with normal full shots, start the downswing with the lead of your lower body; then snap the clubhead downward with a hard slicing motion of your right hand, concentrating on that spot a full 3 inches behind the ball. Be aggressive: Clear out a slice of sand that the ball can ride atop.

Because the club's flange acts as a rudder, it glides through the sand rather than digging into it. The fact that you have this rudder working for you is why you can actually contact the sand so far behind the ball. And the beauty of this is that you will eliminate any possibility of skulling the shot by trying to make contact with the sand too close to the ball.

When you make this right-hand-controlled swing, you'll hit a shot that pops up and out on the target line and lands extremely softly. With a little practice, you'll find that, when necessary, you can drop the ball over the lip of the bunker and stop it next to the tightest pin placements. The main point, though, is that if you follow these sand setup keys accurately, then swing aggressively through the sand with the right-handed action

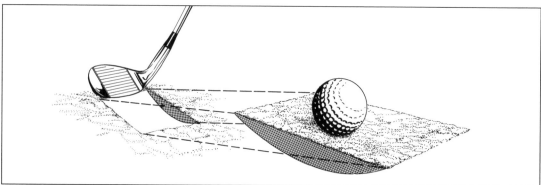

Hit down and through the sand (*above*), the idea being to cut out a slice of sand (*below*).

described, you'll make "skulls" and "left-in-the-bunker" shots a thing of the past, and you'll be able to put that fear of bunkers behind you and start notching some sand saves on your card instead.

Course Management: Play Your Game and Nobody Else's

Let's look down the road a few months and say that you have put in your hard work implementing the full-swing and short-game principles I've described so far. And you're beginning to see some improvements in your shots. You're not standing over the ball on the tee with no clue whether you're going to slice it into the lake on the right or duck-hook it into the trees on the left. You're not standing in the fairway with a 5-iron, not knowing whether your shot will fly 175 yards or 90 yards. You're not skulling pitch shots or leaving the ball in the bunker. True, you're not hitting it like Greg Norman, but you're starting to find a new degree of consistency in your shotmaking.

Now that you've seen these physical improvements begin to happen, it's time to develop your course management skills, and start on the road to becoming a real golfer.

Good course managers plot their course starting from the hole and working back toward the tee. They look at the combination of shots that is most likely to land their ball in the hole in the lowest number of strokes. It's similar to the way expert pool players plan their shots several strokes ahead, giving themselves the best possible "leave" for the next shot they will have to play.

Great course managers are realists. It does no good to simply plan to knock your second shot on a par-four into the hole. You have to look at the hole and ask yourself what is a reasonable goal to accomplish, given the challenge of the particular hole and mixing in an objective awareness of your own ball-striking capabilities. Let's say you're a 12-handicap player. You're facing a solid, 400-yard par-four hole that will require you to hit your drive in the fairway, then a middle or long iron to reach the

Good course managers pick a landing spot in the fairway that will put them in the most strategic position to attack the flag with their approach shot. Here, the ideal route, labeled *1*, is down the left side of the fairway. From this position, the player has a clear path to the hole. If the shot draws slightly, the ball will finish on the green, left of the flag; at worst, it will land just off the left side of the green in the fringe, leaving an easy chip for par.

A smart course manager would never choose the route labeled *2*, even if winding the ball around the dogleg leaves him a shorter shot (because of the angle). The reason is, he now has to negotiate the sand bunkers on the approach. If the ball doesn't draw enough, he faces a sand shot; if it slices, he faces the same shot.

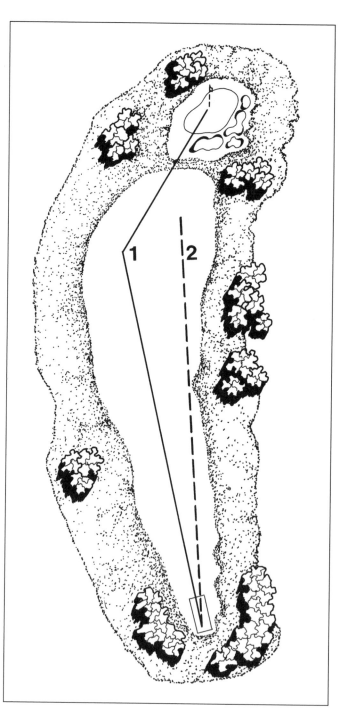

green. This is a hole on which 4, for you, would be a good, helpful score. It is also a reasonable goal for you, something you can definitely accomplish.

Now, let's start at the hole and work backward. Suppose the flag is on the left side of the green, well guarded by a big bunker on the front and left. Let's also say your most consistent shot is a fade, and that a reasonably good drive, which for you is 225 yards, might leave you with about 175 yards, or a 4-iron, to the hole. It's unrealistic to plan to start a 4-iron over the bunker, then fade it in so it finishes "stiff." Yes, you might be able to do it, but to plan on this is the essence of lousy course management. Your goal should simply be to hit this green in regulation—get the ball on the middle or right-center of the green, say between 25 and 40 feet from the hole. From there two putts and a par would be the most likely outcome (although there's nothing that says you can't sink it for birdie, either).

By making the decision that you'd be happy to put the ball on the middle of this green in two, you now begin working backward toward the tee in a manner that is both positive and realistic about your skill level. Let's back up to the fairway landing area. If you had insisted on going for the stick, you would have decided to bring your shot in from the extreme right of the fairway to give you the best angle for this tough pin placement. In aiming for the right side, only a slight error off the tee could have put you in some pretty tough rough. However, since you have decided that you want to shoot for the middle of the green, this means that the position you play from in the fairway is not crucial. Approaching from the middle is fine.

Now we back up to the tee. We've determined that to give you a reasonable chance to hit the green in regulation, all you need to do is hit a moderately good drive in the middle of the fairway. The important thing to remember is, you need a reasonably good drive for you. You do not have to hit a reasonably good drive for Greg Norman. You don't even have to hit a reasonably good drive for the longest hitter in your foursome. You just have to hit a reasonably good drive for you.

I'm making a point of the tee shot in particular because I believe that the *biggest* failure of amateurs in managing their games is that they try to do too much off the tee. They usually try to match the longest drive they've ever hit, off every tee. This is usually disastrous.

Suppose for the sake of argument that a couple of times in your life, when you've had a big wind at your back and the fairways were hard, and you crushed it, you've hit a ball 265 yards, maybe 270. First of all, let's subtract that wind assistance and that hard bounce, and that 270 yards becomes about 245 under normal conditions. That's your true best hit. You should never plan on hitting your driver as hard as you can or as perfectly as you can. (Remember from the ball-striking section, how you're supposed to strive for a backswing that's only three-quarters of your maximum coil?) So, if a tee shot of 245 represents your best hit under normal conditions, what you should be planning to accomplish off the tee is a shot that travels 20 yards shorter than your Sunday punch—in this example, about 225 yards.

By following this realistic approach to what you want to accomplish, you take a lot of pressure off yourself on the tee. You know you don't have to hit your best drive to get home in two. You know you don't have to hit the ball down the right side of the fairway and obtain a perfect angle to the flag to hit this green in regulation. By setting a realistic goal off the tee, you've given yourself the greatest possible chance to make a free, relaxed, unforced swing—and increase the percentages that you'll execute the tee shot well. Maybe you'll catch the driver just perfectly and hit it 245 yards, so you have only a 6-iron in. If so, great. Maybe you'll catch the drive less solidly than average, and fade it into the rough, leaving yourself a 190-yard 5-wood shot. If so, that's not the end of the world either. You might still be able to lie two on the green.

If you learn to think this way, to play within yourself, to plan for a little less than your career shots as you work your way around the entire course, you'll be amazed at how much more you feel you're in control of your golf round. You'll find that you can get positive surprises during a round, rather than just all negative ones. For example, you might find yourself making extra-good contact with the driver, so that you're hitting a club less than usual to the greens. Or you may find that the greens

Perhaps the second biggest negative I see in course management by amateurs is that they're too concerned about what club they "should" be hitting into a certain hole. Maybe there's a par four on their course and they heard, "Joe got home on 14 with a drive and a wedge." So the amateur thinks, "Gee, I'd like to get home with a wedge there, too—at the very least, I should be able to get home with an 8- or 9-iron." Or they think they should hit a 6-iron into a 180-yard par three just because they heard somebody else did.

There's no room for this kind of thinking in professional course management—and there is no excuse for any golfer being unprofessional in the area of course management. What club you need to reach any given green means next to nothing. As my dad always said, "There is no place on a scorecard for what club you hit, only a box for your score."

Why do you think you are allowed to carry fourteen clubs? It's so you can select the club *you* need to hit the ball to your intended target. To think in terms of what you'd "like" to get home with is lousy course management, plain and simple.

Take it from me—the Tour pros couldn't care less what the other players in their threesome are hitting. To them, the various clubs are like surgical tools to a surgeon. The numbers on the clubs simply represent an angle of clubface loft on each of those "tools"—and they are only interested in using the tool they can swing in a controlled fashion, in order to drop the ball next to the cup. Start thinking this way right now and leave all the crowing about reaching the 14th with a drive and a wedge to others.

superintendent woke up in a generous mood and placed most of the flags in the middle of greens, so you can aim directly for more flags than usual and, if you execute well, have more good putts at birdies than average.

DEAD CENTER OF THE FAIRWAY IS FINE

Unless your name happens to be Ben Hogan or Lee Trevino, one of the best pieces of course management advice I can give you is to try to put all your tee shots into the center of the fairway.

Let's face it—if you are an amateur player, you are not going to be so accurate with the driver (or 3-wood) that you can consistently place the ball in a certain segment of the fairway. And let me tell you a secret: most of the PGA Tour pros aren't that accurate either. Most of them aim for the center of the fairway and try to keep themselves as far away from potential trouble as possible. So should you.

Besides the fact that the center of the fairway is the farthest point from trouble, let's think about this also—how many holes will you play where you will face a very difficult shot to the pin from the center of the fairway? Sure, if the pin is tucked tightly behind a bunker on the right side, you have a slight advantage coming in from the left rather than the center, and vice versa. But particularly on the courses you play, which are not set up for PGA Tour events, you're not going to see too many pins that are really "tucked."

Except for unusual holes or circumstances, I recommend that all amateur players make it a policy to aim for the center of the fairway with their tee shots. This simple rule will take a lot of pressure off your tee shot swing and, I believe, allow you to make better contact and hit the ball straighter to begin with.

The only time I recommend that the handicap player not aim down the middle is, not for the purpose of gaining a great angle to the pin, but rather to make sure to avoid major problems off the tee. Let's say you're playing a par-four hole that has out-of-bounds all the way down the left side, about ten yards from the fairway. To the right is moderate rough, with no trees or other major concerns. In situations like this, it's intelligent course management to shift your aim from the center of the fairway to the right side of the fairway. Simply aim ten yards farther right than normal. While this increases the chance that a slight push may end up in the right rough, you already know that that is not a severe penalty. Meanwhile, should you pull or hook the shot some, giving yourself this extra ten-yard "safety net" will probably keep you in bounds, or possibly even in the fairway.

Remember, I only recommend this tactic when you have a severe penalty on one side of the fairway and a very minimal one on the other. Nine times out of ten, the smartest strategy is the simplest one: play for the middle of the fairway.

As my dad used to say, "On every shot, you need a plan of attack that starts out with a clear picture of the shot you're trying to play, a shot you've already rehearsed in your mind's eye."

Before you step up to any shot—be it a drive, approach, short-game shot, or putt—you should stand behind the ball and imagine the exact flight or roll you are hoping to achieve. I cannot stress enough how important good visualization is. You must have a picture in your mind, as you stand over the ball, of what the golf ball is going to do. If you don't have that picture, you're likely to hit generally haphazard shots or, perhaps worse, start overconcentrating on a variety of swing cues, thus confusing yourself prior to the swing.

I believe Jack Nicklaus is the best ever at previewing perfect golf shots and then trusting his body and his senses to recreate these shots. Greg Norman is great at this too, although I think Nicklaus had the ability to do this all through his career, while Greg has had to improve at it over the years.

Make a pact with yourself that you will never step up to a shot without first seeing the exact flight, landing, and roll in your mind's eye. If you make this an automatic part of your shot-planning discipline, I believe it will influence your body to put into action what you've seen with your mind.

"COURSE SMARTS"—LEARNING THE FINE POINTS OF COURSE MANAGEMENT AND THE MENTAL GAME CAN HELP YOU THINK YOUR WAY TO LOWER SCORES

Unless you've been playing this game for many years and have practiced every aspect of the game—driving, fairway wood play, medium irons, trouble shots, short game, sand play, and putting—you probably don't play scratch golf. Don't think, however, that because you haven't had the time to work hard on your game, or probably never will be able to devote hours and hours to practice, you can't improve your score. In fact, you can save numerous shots per round simply by learning the fine points of course management.

Three of my top students—Greg Norman, Davis Love III, and Tiger

Woods—all possess "course smarts," and continue to learn more each day about the importance of course management and the mental side of golf—which, when all the fat is boiled off, simply means that they are experts at playing the percentages. Rarely during a round does any one of these players "give" shots away. They are all intelligent course managers who realize that the art of scoring has more to do with what goes on between the ears than how pretty their swing looks on video or in front of a mirror. In other words, they think their way to lower scores by reading the lie, carefully analyzing the course situation, picking the right club, and concentrating hard on the shot they intend to play.

To the typical high-handicap player, the immediate choice of club to use off the tee on a par-four or par-five hole is always the driver, no matter what the conditions may be. The hole can be narrow, the hole can be short, the hole can feature an exaggerated sloping fairway, the wind can be blowing hard in the player's face, there can be water down the left side, or woods on the right. Still, in reading the scorecard and seeing the hole's length, the average player assumes that the driver is the one and only club for the job, as though the only goal on every tee is to hit the ball as far as possible down the fairway. The pro or top amateur player, skilled in the fine points of course management, knows that there are many factors to consider beyond distance in choosing the proper club.

Let's now take a look at the fine points of course management so that you, too, can learn how to shoot low scores without making drastic swing changes or devoting long hours each week to practice.

PLAY THE SLOPES

One major reason why Greg Norman finished at the top of the PGA Tour money list in 1995 is his keen ability to "read" a course.

Let's take Augusta National as an example, the course on which the Masters is played every year, and where "The Shark" has had great success.

The 10th hole at Augusta is 485 yards in length. Technically, any hole over 475 yards is a par five, but during the Masters championship the pros play this hole as a par four. The hole curves or "doglegs" left, and features a huge slope that's located in the middle of the fairway about 230 yards from the tee. On the far side of this slope, the fairway flattens out.

I would be willing to bet you that nine out of ten amateurs playing this course for the first time would automatically select the driver. Not Greg Norman. Greg realizes that if he were to hit a driver, the ball would carry the slope, land on the flat spot of the fairway, then stop very quickly, leaving him a long shot into the green. Greg hits a 3-wood in this situation. This club allows him to land the ball on the slope, so that it bounces off the contoured fairway, then zooms forward as much as 100 yards. The total distance he hits the ball is 330 yards—with a 3-wood! Now he's left with a much shorter approach shot into the green than he would have faced had he selected a driver off the tee.

Another reason why the 3-wood is the smart play for Greg, on this hole, is that a driver hit off-line to the right will run through the fairway and come to rest among tall pines. Not the spot you want to be on Augusta's 10th hole. From there, bogey or worse is a near certainty.

Whether or not you hit the ball as far as Greg Norman, or whether you ever play Augusta National, you can still learn these valuable lessons about managing your game sensibly:

- Before selecting a driver, look at the contour of the fairway of the hole you're playing. If there's a downslope you can use as a springboard to extra distance, as there is on the 10th hole of Augusta National, and you can reach it with a 3-wood, use that club to your advantage.
- If you can't reach the slope, select a 3-wood anyway. Even with a driver you'll probably never reach the flat spot of the fairway, located past the slope. As a result, you'll be playing your second shot, and a very long one at that, from a downhill lie; for even the seasoned player, this is one of the toughest shots to hit powerfully and accurately. Chances are, if you're forced to play this shot, the ball will shoot dead right into trouble, resulting in wasted strokes and an overall higher score at the end of the day. If you don't reach the

slope with a 3-wood, you will have a level lie on the fairway, and still be in position to hit a very accurate and powerful second shot. Now, lying 2, you're all set to hit a short iron onto the green, then either one-putt for a score of 4, or two-putt for a 5. Remember that in normal circumstances, this 485-yard hole would be considered a par five. Therefore, at worst you will score a par; at best a birdie—and you've greatly reduced your chance of going for a big number.

- The same benefits of hitting a 3-wood on a sharp dogleg left apply to the long hitter. You know from this example that you will gain more distance with a 3-wood. Moreover, if you slice the ball with the 3-wood, or hit your tee shot a little off line to the right, it won't reach the trees. You will still be in a position to make your par.

LET THE COURSE CONDITIONS HELP YOU

Another valuable lesson about playing smart tee shots can be learned from Tiger Woods, the young superstar who won his second consecutive U.S. Amateur championship in 1995 at the Newport Country Club in Rhode Island.

During practice rounds before the event, Tiger noticed that the fairways were dried out, due to a virtual drought. He also noticed that wind seemed to be a constant factor at this prestigious venue. Moreover, on most holes, the wind blew directly at the player.

When the event began, the conditions remained the same. In the end, Tiger prevailed—largely because he was a smart course manager.

Tiger discovered that by playing a 2-iron off the tee, and hitting a draw shot, he could get enough roll on the hard fairways to make up for what he lost in carry. The 2-iron also gave him more control to keep the ball in play in the windy conditions. Tiger actually hit his 2-iron tee shots an average distance of 290 yards.

His advantages didn't just come on the holes into the wind, where opponents who hit drives were adversely affected. On the 3rd hole, which measures around 365 yards, the wind was at his back during one of his matches. His opponent, who played a driver, hit the ball "too far," into trouble. Not Tiger—he took out his trusty 2-iron and drove the green. Needless to say, he won the hole and that match.

Your Lesson:

On a fast running course, with the wind in your face or at your back, often a 2-iron draw shot is a smarter play than swinging away with a driver.

PLAY TO YOUR STRENGTHS

One common thread in the thinking processes of most amateur players is an overaggressive approach to the game. Take the ultimate trouble situation: You are among trees, 170 yards from a green that's guarded by a bunker in front of it and thick rough to the sides and back of it.

In this situation, the typical club-level player, who believes that "trees are 90 percent air," is going to go for broke. He or she is going to try to hit a low rising shot between the branches, hoping that the ball will rise above the next tree directly in line, carry to the green, then land next to the pin. Don't get me wrong, before swinging you should always visualize a positive result. However, in situations such as this, if you want to shoot the lowest possible score, you should not visualize a miracle shot. Frankly, the odds of missing the trees and hitting the ball close to the hole—or anywhere on the green—are slim to none.

The good player, be it a top pro or low-handicap amateur, takes a wayward tee shot in stride. Then he or she conjures up a sensible mental strategy for scoring either a tough earned par or a bogey. No worse.

In order to accomplish the ideal goal of scoring par, the golfer must play to his or her strengths—a strategy my dad taught me a lot about.

In this situation, my dad would tell the golfer to consider three recovery routes that, in the end, would allow the player to save par.

1. If the route directly to the hole was blocked by branches, and it was too risky to hit a low boring straight shot, he'd tell the player to aim

at a gap farther left of target, and hit a low fade around the trees down the fairway. That's if the fade was the player's strongest suit.

2. If he thought the player could thread the shot through the branches of a nearby tree, but couldn't get the ball to carry a second tree directly in line with the hole, he'd recommend that the player hit a low shot all the way to the sand trap in front of the green. That's if the player's strongest suit was bunker play.

3. If the student was a high handicapper, he'd recommend that the player choose a wide opening between the trees, then a short or middle iron shot, out sideways, into the middle of the fairway. At least then the student could hit the green on his third shot, and either sink a long putt for par, or two-putt for bogey.

Your Lesson:

Play to your strengths and keep in mind that after a bad tee shot, bogey is not so bad a score.

PLAY THE STRONGER CLUB

If there's one thing that often gets in the way of a player's ability to shoot the lowest possible score on a hole, it's the ego. Almost all golfers like to brag about hitting a wedge into a par-four hole. That's a big mistake. A good course manager always swings the stronger club. Let me explain, using Davis Love as the ultimate example.

One reason why Davis is playing winning golf these days is a mature approach to club selection. Like all young players, he got caught up in the distance thing early on in his career, maybe because he's human like all of us, or maybe because the golf press likes to hear about his magnificent on-course power feats. Whatever the reason, Davis, as I said, has grown up. He's learned that trying to hit a shorter club into a hole ruins your game. Let me explain the reasons why.

Let's say, on a short par-four hole, you select a wedge for a shot that really requires you to play an 8-iron. Now you will have to swing the club back farther at a faster tempo. In turn, this sloppy, out-of-control, quick swing is going to cause you to lose your balance, with the end result being a mishit shot. Usually, you'll hit the ball "fat" or "thin," depending on the arc of your swing. Either way, you're going to have to hit an awfully good third shot in order to save par.

The smart strategy, and one that's turned Davis's game around, is his ability to take a stronger, less lofted club than the one he would usually hit from a designated distance. In the situation just cited, Davis would play a 7-iron and make a smooth three-quarter swing. By taking the stronger club and making a shorter swing, he has full control of his body movements and the club. Furthermore, if he doesn't hit the ball as solidly as he should, the ball will still find the front of the green. If he hits it real pure, the ball will fly over the green, where most of the time there's little trouble.

Your Lesson:

Swing within yourself. Never take a weaker club and try to kill it, just so you can tell your friends, over a drink at the 19th hole, about your heroic feat. For every one of these great tales, there are stories of failure. You may not tell your friends about them, but you know only too well, at the end of the day, that several "ego shots" ruined your score.

DON'T REACH FOR YOUR FAVORITE CHIPPING CLUB ALL OF THE TIME

The top-notch player knows that different lies around the green call for different clubs. For that reason, he or she has no favorite club. It's just a question of what club is the best for the situation at hand. Sometimes this could be a wedge; other times this could be a 2-iron or any one of the irons in your bag.

I'm very proud of Greg Norman, because of how hard he's worked to become a greenside virtuoso. Years ago, he didn't have half the chip shots in his bag that he has now. He'll tell you himself that the simple reason was, he didn't practice the chipping game that much, neglecting it to work on driving and other parts of the full-shot game.

When Greg analyzed his game, he quickly faced one hard fact that every golfer should pay attention to: In order to reach your full potential as a player, whether on tour or at your local club, you have got to learn how to hit a variety of shots with a variety of clubs from around the green.

Some players try to hit almost all of their greenside chip shots with a wedge. These clubs, whether they're pitching, sand, or lob, work fine if the ball is sitting up in the fringe and the shot is relatively short. However, other lies and situations require different strategies. For example, when the ball is sitting up and the pin is on the top tier of a green, say 40 feet away, you're better off playing a medium iron. When the chip shot is in the 100-foot range, you're better off playing a long iron. The list of different lies that call for different clubs goes on and on, and the only way to learn how to handle these various chip shot situations is by hitting shots out of different lies to holes set out at various distances. You'd be surprised how much you can learn about the art of chipping just by devoting one day to solid practice.

From my own experience, teaching the members at Lochinvar Golf Club and playing with amateurs around the world, I found that they, too, like to play the majority of shots with a favorite club, usually a pitching wedge or 7-iron. This is one way why they waste shots around the green. Don't you make the same on-course error.

Remember, one of the fine points of good course management is knowing what club to play, not only when hitting shots off the tee or into the green, but when you're chipping. Therefore, learn to develop a strong repertoire of shots. That way, when you hit your ball in the fringe, you can quickly determine what club will allow you to recover from a particular type of lie and hit the ball close enough to the hole for an easy one-putt par conversion.

BE SMART WHEN PLAYING FROM SAND

Finding your ball in a fairway bunker is not a pleasant sight, particularly if it was the result of a bad bounce or your not hitting the ball quite far enough to carry the hazard. All the same, part of the game is accepting a troublesome lie and using common sense to deal with it. Having said this, club players often become so ticked off about landing in a fairway bunker that they will attempt to hit a wooden club over a high lip, with the pipe dream of landing the ball next to the hole. You may hit that one great shot, but over time you will pay a dear price, in terms of how many shots you throw away.

Whenever you land in a fairway bunker that features a high lip between your ball and the hole, don't throw caution to the wind and reach for a wood. Accept the fact that you hit a bad shot or got a bad break, and get down to business.

The smart strategy in this situation is to play a medium iron, or even a more lofted club, with your priorities being to hit the ball over the lip, while at the same time advancing the ball as far down the fairway as possible. For example, if the distance to the green calls for a 5-iron, but the lip is relatively high, play a 7-iron and aim to put yourself in position to save par with a good pitch and putt.

Greg Norman has won two British Open titles because he's never played a silly shot from a fairway bunker. And, trust me, he's been in many while playing the links courses of Scotland and England.

I realize that sometimes it's tempting to take a big risk. But overall, it's not worth it. Even the great Jack Nicklaus has learned that lesson. During the 1995 British Open, played at St. Andrews, he gambled out of a fairway bunker and took several shots to get out. And if the "Golden Bear" can't hit the miracle shot from one of these hazards, chances are you can't.

FINE-TUNE YOUR COURSE MANAGEMENT

How you manage your golf game will necessarily vary from most other players' course management approaches. And your own approach to managing your game should change over time, as the physical aspects of your game change. If you use the swing tenets I've described and work diligently at them for, say, a year or more, you will be a much more consistent ball striker than you are now. You might also possess a short game in which you have much greater confidence to bail you out of trouble.

These improvements, of course, point toward adopting a more aggressive strategy for course management.

On the other hand, there are senior players who, unfortunately, do not have the strength and suppleness to swing the club as powerfully as they once did. They may be more particularly limited in escaping from trouble—deep rough and deep bunkers—than they were in years past. This doesn't mean that they can't still play well, but it does mean that a shift to a more conservative course management strategy will be the best thing for their game.

My main point to you is, always be aware of what your strong suits and your weak areas are. Of course, you'll always be striving to improve those weak areas, but for now you must plan your game so that you play to your strengths, not your weak areas. Say, for example, you are not yet a good bunker player, and the greens at your course are fairly well trapped. Let's also say you are a pretty good chipper. You should shade your approach shots so that if you miss the green, you're likely to have a relatively simple chip shot rather than a bunker shot you really don't want. If the bunker is to the left, shade to the right slightly. If the bunker is in front, take a little extra club, so if anything you're chipping from the back fringe.

Good course management is not all about playing safe, by the way. Suppose you are very consistent and have good feel with your short irons—the 8, the 9, and the wedges. You feel confident you are going to stick shots with these clubs within 20 feet of the flag virtually every time, sometimes very close. If this is the case, use your strength. Attack with these clubs and shade your shots toward the fat of the green with the middle and long irons.

How is your putting touch currently? Unless you consider yourself a great and fearless putter, you should take into consideration the types of putts that various shots into the greens are likely to leave you with. Particularly if you play on fast, contoured surfaces, try to plan your approaches so that, if you execute as you hope, you'll leave yourself with a fairly straight, uphill putt. Believe me, this type of awareness and planning can work wonders for your putting totals, without your even improving your stroke.

A golf course doesn't always play the same way. In late spring, when the grass is growing as fast as it will at any time of the year, you may find that the rough is pretty hard to play from. This may call for an adjustment in strategy in which you pull a 3- or 4-wood out of the bag more frequently, sacrificing a little distance off the tee to increase your odds of hitting your approach from the short grass. Conversely, in mid to late summer, you may find that the course is dried out and the rough is not as much of a threat. If this is the case, your planning from the tee can become a little more aggressive than usual.

Air humidity and temperature changes are always factors to consider. A shot to a 165-yard par-three on a damp day with the temperature around 50 degrees may require that you hit at least a 4-iron. Exactly the same shot under clear, dry conditions with the temperature at 80 may mean that a 6-iron is the club.

As important as it is to take into account the elements of nature, it is equally important to take yourself into account as well. Some days you will feel relaxed, loose, and limber. The clubs feel light in your hands, and you've hit the ball solidly and long during your warm-ups. Great! Perhaps you can go with the shorter of two clubs whenever you have any doubt about which club to use.

Other days, you may not be quite at your best. Perhaps you had to work overtime during the week, didn't get as much rest as usual, and your body's feeling it. Or you have a cold, or the weather is chilly and windy and you just can't get loose. All these conditions are things that the smart course manager takes into consideration in playing the game that day. Does this mean that you assume that you're not going to play well? Absolutely not. All this means is that you're going to play perhaps a little more conservatively. Plan to play a little farther away from the real trouble spots. Perhaps, after hitting your warm-up shots, you'll decide that, generally speaking, you'll go with one more club today than you would normally. That you'll play more toward the fat of the greens and take two-putt pars, considering any birdies a bonus.

Let me tell you something. The top PGA Tour pros play perhaps one hundred competitive rounds a year, not counting practice and pro-am rounds. They travel the entire country and sometimes the world, playing in different time zones almost every week. Do you think they feel great every day? Of course not. Do you think they recognize where their own metabolism stands on a given day, and take it into account in planning their upcoming round? Of course they do. This is all part of being a professional course manager.

If you take this awareness of your limitations on any given day into account, and adjust your strategic game accordingly, you'll be surprised at the kind of scores you can shoot—even when you're not feeling your very best.

Physical Conditioning—The Fourth Cornerstone of Winning Golf

At this point, you understand what you need to do in the setup and swing in order to improve your ball striking. You know the basics of good short-game execution so that, with continued practice, you'll become more and more capable of saving par. And you've learned an approach to the mental side and to course management that should help you get the most out of your game, whether you're at your physical peak or struggling with your swing.

Let's conclude this section with a factor in everyone's play that's often overlooked. It is not about the actual technique of hitting any given golf shot, nor is it about the strategy of playing various shots. I'm referring to your physical conditioning and how it can affect your game.

As I mentioned at the outset, I consider physical conditioning the fourth cornerstone of winning golf because it influences how you play every shot and, I believe, how well you think about every shot. Let's be very honest here: If you are a relatively sedentary person, working in an office five days a week and riding a golf cart the once or twice a week that you play, you can't possibly hit the golf shots that, say, Greg Norman hits. You are not physically prepared to do so.

Now I realize it's not every reader's goal to strike the ball and play the game at that world-class level. However, there are an awful lot of golf shots that you will be able to execute if you are physically supple and strong that you simply won't be able to execute if you're in poor condition. It's not only the distance you can hit the ball that is affected by your physical conditioning, it's your ability to stay in balance throughout the swing; it's also your ability to dig the ball out of heavy rough, to play the ball from buried lies in bunkers, to make the physical in-swing adjustments needed to hit the ball low in the wind or high to a well-guarded pin. Your physical condition also affects your feel in the short game, your ability to read greens, and your ability to concentrate on every shot at a high level. Finally, if you're in shape, you'll find that walking an 18-hole round, even on a hilly course, will not be difficult for you—and walking the course is definitely the best way to play the game.

I'm going to provide you with a workout regimen that will help you specifically in stretching and strengthening the body parts that need it most in order for you to play your best. Note that this is not intended to be a complete physical training regimen for all types of athletes (although doing the exercises shown here would probably be helpful to almost anybody).

I'm going to make a recommendation here that, I suspect, is not going to be a very popular one, but if you're serious about improving, you should follow it. I recommend that you set up an exercise system in which you do some or all of the exercises described for a minimum of ten minutes per day, seven days a week. Yes, you heard me! I want you to perform these exercises every single day, for at least ten minutes. You'll find that you can't do all of these exercises with the minimum number of repetitions suggested in ten minutes. Feel free to break up the exercises any way you want, as long as you alternate them so that you are continually doing all of them in a sequence.

There's a specific reason I would like you to commit to doing these every day, if only for a short period of time. It's because I want you to make it a habit, a part of your daily routine just like taking a shower or brushing your teeth. I could have suggested that you do all of these exercises, which might take thirty to forty minutes, every other day or even twice a week. That would actually add up to even more physical conditioning time. However, people have a tendency to start out doing something three times a week, but then, a couple of months later, they're doing it just once a week, or not at all. I'd rather see you make a commitment to a short period of time every day.

You may not be able to get to a golf course or driving range every day, but you can do these exercises with virtually no equipment in your own home. Make the commitment to doing these either first thing in the morning or last thing at night, for ten minutes, and soon you'll benefit on the course and feel better in general, too.

STRETCHING THE GOLF MUSCLES

While stretching and strengthening of the muscles are somewhat interrelated, I'm going to break down these exercises based on whether their prime function is to stretch or to strengthen. Let's look at stretching those golf muscles first, because not only will these exercises

The Torso Twist:
from start to finish.

improve your overall ability to swing the club, they will greatly reduce the chance of injury either on or off the course.

Torso Twist:

Take a golf club and, holding it with one hand near each end, place it behind your back or neck. Stand upright, then bend your knees just slightly. Next, squeeze, or tighten, your abdominal muscles. Then, while breathing normally, slowly turn your entire torso to the right; hold, then turn your torso slowly but fully to the left. Keep the abdominals tight as you continue the exercise. Starting out, do this exercise for one minute, or about ten repetitions in both directions. As with all these exercises, you can increase the number of repetitions until you are doing the torso twist for a total of two minutes.

Knees to Chest:

This is an excellent exercise to stretch the lower back, and is a great precaution against injury to this critical area. Lie down on your back,

with your feet flat on the floor and your knees up. Reach with your arms and clasp your hands around your knees. Next, pull your knees up to your chest and hold them there for a count of ten. Relax your hands and let your knees and feet back down. Repeat this exercise a total of three times for starters: it will take about one minute. After you've done this several times, increase the number of repetitions to five; this should take a total of no more than two minutes.

As an alternate exercise, try the single knee to chest. Keep one leg extended flat along the floor, then grasp around the other knee with both hands, and pull it up to the chest. Hold it for a count of ten. Repeat the exercise three times with one leg, then switch legs, again holding for three counts of ten.

Hip Stretch:

This is a great exercise to add flexibility to the hip muscles and tendons, which are in an area of the physique where added flexibility can really increase the power in your swing.

Again, lie on your back with your knees bent and your feet flat on the floor. Cross your left leg over your right so that the ankle is just outside your right kneecap. Reach with both arms around your bent right leg, and pull both legs toward the chest. Hold this strength for ten seconds, then repeat a total of three times. Next, switch legs so that you are crossing your right leg over your flexed left leg. Again, pull both legs up from this position and hold for three sets of ten seconds each.

Trunk Stretch:

Lie on your back, with your legs straight. Bend your left knee upward, then cross it over your right leg, placing your left foot to the outside of your right knee. Reach your left arm straight out along the floor. Finally, put your right hand on the outside of the left knee, then slowly pull your left knee over to the right, all the while keeping your extended left arm and shoulder on the floor. You may have to struggle to do this at first, because there will be a strain on the outside of the left hip and in the lower back. It will get easier with time. Do your best to hold this stretch for ten seconds, then repeat a total of three times. Then switch the process so that your left leg is extended and your right leg is crossed over your left, with your right arm extended. Again, repeat the hold for three counts of ten.

Upper Back Stretch:

Here's a good one to get your upper back muscles in tune, along with the deltoid muscles of your upper arms. It's simple. Clasp your fingers behind your head, so that your elbows are forward in your field of vision. Slowly pull your elbows back so that they are extended back fully, parallel to your shoulders. Hold them there for a count of five, feeling the stretch along your upper back. Repeat this stretch a total of ten times.

Here's an alternative to this exercise that you can do to add a little extra resistance as your upper back muscles develop. Do this exercise in the same manner, except that instead of clasping your hands behind your head, hold light weights in each hand behind your head, about three to five pounds each.

STRENGTHENING THE GOLF MUSCLES

There is no substitute for having strong golf muscles. There are so many situations on the golf course where increased strength (combined with suppleness, of course, so that your strength can be channeled into a smooth, free-flowing swing action) will help you to execute the swing as it needs to be executed in order to hit top-class golf shots.

You might think that when I say most golfers will benefit from increased strength I mean that they will hit the ball longer. That's only one benefit, and it's probably not the most important one. If you can become physically stronger, the greatest advantage is that you'll be able to play shots from trouble much more effectively. I'm referring to shots out of deep rough, playing the ball out of a divot or a depression, having the ability to hit the ball low from under trees, yet make it carry a good distance, and so on. Increased strength will also be a significant factor in bad weather, either in rain, when the course is playing very long, or in cold weather, when the ball won't carry as far as normal.

Some of you readers may play a lot of golf and do strength exercises already, but I would guess, from most of the amateurs I teach, that most of you will also benefit from some strength building. So here are some drills to put into your daily workout routine.

Swing a Medicine Ball:

This is an exercise that Greg Norman does religiously. Greg has a medicine ball, which you can get at most sporting goods stores. It's a little larger than a basketball and weighs about seven pounds.

Hold the medicine ball in front of you, so you're in a posture similar to the address position for a golf shot. Slowly, swing the medicine ball back and through, just as though you were swinging a club. Make sure that you swing the medicine ball with your torso, not with your hands and arms. Simply hold onto the ball and make a turning motion with your torso, just as you would during a proper golf swing.

You don't have to swing the ball very far at first—it's okay if your hands move only to hip height or waist height at first. Swing the medicine ball back and forth with your torso, slowly, about twenty times or for one minute. If you do this exercise correctly, you will feel it in your abdomen.

Gradually you'll find that you're able to extend your turn farther, so that your hands and the middle of the ball are about level with your rib cage. That's great. However, always remember to control the motion with your midsection rather than making the ball move with your arms.

The main benefit of this exercise is that you will really strengthen and tighten that abdomen. Most of us could use that, wouldn't you say? There sure aren't too many 41-year-olds with as trim a waist as Greg Norman's. In addition, your hands and forearms will get a great workout. Even though you won't actively "swing" the medicine ball with your hands and arms, they must support the weight of the ball from the sides, not from underneath, throughout the exercise. This will definitely strengthen them as well.

Swing a Weighted Club:

This exercise is a close substitute to swinging a medicine ball. Simply take an old club (preferably a wood) that you don't use anymore and add a fairly small amount of weight to it. You can do this in one of several ways. You can remove the grip and simply pour sand down the shaft, then replace the grip (making sure to plug the small hole at the top of the grip so the sand doesn't spill out). Or you can add weight to the clubhead, either in the form of one or more "doughnuts" that you can slip down over the neck of the club, or by simply wrapping the clubhead with heavy lead tape.

You don't have to add a lot of weight to a club to make it an effective strengthening tool, by the way. You should start light and make sure you don't strain any muscles by overdoing it on the first try. Believe it or not, the addition of 10 to 12 ounces of weight, particularly if it's attached to the clubhead, will make swinging the club a surprisingly good workout for most golfers.

Set up with your heavy club as if to play a normal shot. Then make a slow backswing turn, striving to use your torso as described in the medicine ball drill. Stop at the top, pause, then make a slow, smooth downswing, concentrating on using your entire left side to lead the club down. Continue on to a nice balanced follow-through. In this exercise you must always control the clubhead. Don't swing so hard that the clubhead carries you on the downswing. You must control the clubhead in order to build strength.

Make sure to keep the entire swing slow, so that each swing takes about three seconds. Make 20 to 25 practice swings for starters, then build up if you like. Some of you will also find that after trying this a few times, you can control a slightly heavier club. If so, add some weight, but do it gradually, in increments of several ounces at a time.

This exercise has similar benefits to the medicine ball drill. However, because the weight is farther away from you, in the clubhead, you may find that there's more stress on (and therefore more strengthening of) your hands and forearms, and a little less on your torso, than with the medicine ball.

Arm and Leg Reach:

This is a great exercise to strengthen what are known as the extensor muscles in your lower back. Get on the floor, on your hands and knees. (This exercise will definitely be more comfortable if you can do it on a thick carpet or some type of padding.) From this position, raise your right arm straight out in front of you, parallel to the ground, then stretch your left leg out behind you. Try to hold this position for a count of five (which may not be as easy as it sounds—you may find it difficult to keep your balance!). Lower your arm and leg and repeat five times for that count of five. Next, reverse the procedure so that you're extending your left arm and your right leg. Again, hold the position for a count of five, lower the arm and leg, and repeat five times.

This exercise will help increase your torso turn through the swing, and also provide insurance against back injury.

Use a Stair Climber:

A major source of distance is your thighs and, quite frankly, your rear end. The hamstrings and the gluteus maximus are the biggest muscles in the body. If you can build these up, then use them correctly at the start of the downswing, you can really add a lot of length to all of your shots.

A stair climber, which is now a staple item at almost all health clubs, is a great device for building these muscles. If you have not seen one, it is a boxlike apparatus that houses the machinery to which two foot pedals and two hand rails are attached. You step onto these foot pedals and push down on them alternately with each foot, against the machine's resistance. The pedals are attached in such a way that you can push them down just a couple of inches, so that you don't feel too much resistance, or you can push them down a foot or more. When you push down as far as you can, you will really feel it in your thighs and rear end.

Using the stair climber is a tiring exercise. It's hard to tell any individual how hard to push, or how long to stay on the stair climber, because it is also an aerobic activity that will elevate your heart rate. Some people will be able to stay on it for a number of minutes; others may find themselves worn out (at first) in just a minute or so. Of course, you'll quickly be able to increase your time if you stick with it.

If you have never used a StairMaster or Versa Climber, I strongly recommend that you take it slow at first. Get the feel of the machine. Make sure that if you begin to feel at all weak or faint, you stop immediately. That aside, working on one will be great for your full swing.

If you don't have access to a health club, remember that everyone has access to stairs. Climbing several flights of stairs briskly is a great exercise, too. Its only disadvantage is that as you make each step up (which is the equivalent of a step down on the StairMaster), you don't have the soft resistance to each step that the machine provides. Still, climbing regular stairs will help you. In addition to your daily exercise routine, I recommend that you get into the habit of climbing stairs whenever you have the opportunity, instead of using an elevator.

Develop Your Hands and Wrists:
Last, if you want to improve your swing strength, you must increase the strength in your hands and wrists. Strong hands and wrists in and of themselves may not add raw distance to your shots, but having them will help you in two crucial areas of shotmaking:

1. Controlling Your Mishits: Whenever you contact a ball away from the sweet spot, the club is going to twist, to some degree, in your hands during impact. For example, if you hit one way off the toe, the clubface will twist open and the ball will start way right.

    The stronger your hands and forearms, the better you will be able to resist the twisting that occurs on off-center shots. This will prove a tremendous aid to keeping the ball in play when you are not swinging your best, and will vastly increase your chances of grinding out a good score.

2. Getting Out of the Rough: The stronger your hands and forearms, the better you will be able to power the ball out of long grass, wet grass, weeds, any type of really deep lie. There are some lies, such as in the dreaded ice plant that grows on the courses of the Monterey peninsula in California, where if you don't have a lot of hand strength to keep the clubhead moving, you can't even get the ball out. That's an extreme example, but there are many situations where the player with weaker hands and forearms might only be able to chop the ball 25 yards back into the fairway with a sand wedge. If you have strong hands and forearms, you might be able to use a 7- or 8-iron and advance the ball close to, if not all the way to, the green.

That said, there are some simple ways to increase your hand and forearm strength. First, get a set of hand grips, which you can purchase at any sporting goods store. Sometimes hand grips are available with different tension settings. If you know you are relatively weak in this area, don't buy the grips with the highest tension.

Simply get into the habit of squeezing the grips a little bit every day, doing an equal number of repetitions with each hand. You might find that, at first, you can do only 10 squeezes before your hand is too fatigued to close the handle. That's fine, don't worry about it. Just keep at it. See if you can make it to 15 squeezes at a time, then 20. Keep your hand grips handy, even carrying them in your briefcase so that you can do a few extra squeezes at the office during off moments.

An alternative to hand grips is a rubber "squeeze ball." These are usually slightly bigger than a pool cue ball and a little smaller than a baseball. The squeeze ball may not provide quite as much resistance as the grips, so you'll probably be able to do more repetitions. Make sure to squeeze the ball in such a way that you get the pinkie finger into the action. If the ball is not large enough, you'll tend to exercise only the index, middle and ring fingers.

Keeping your hand strength up is something you'll gradually start to do unconsciously. Over the course of a few months, you will notice that you're escaping the rough better and your worst hits are not flying as wildly as before.

Like Father,

CHAPTER THREE

Like Son

THE SWING SECRETS

AND SPECIALTY SHOTS

MY DAD TAUGHT ME

Family albums usually contain photographs of the Grand Canyon, Fourth of July block parties or picnics, Niagara Falls, favorite cats and dogs, brothers in baby carriages, sisters in cap and gown, big fish caught off Montauk Point or at some exotic Caribbean island, classic cars or old bombs that just got you around, sons in Little League uniforms, daughters selling Girl Scout cookies, and keepsakes like that.

In my family album, and those belonging to all three of my brothers, practically all you find are photographs of adults and young people playing golf. Furthermore, they contain memorabilia that remind us of the person who was most responsible for the Harmons getting so immersed in this great game. To you, that man is just a name—Claude Harmon, Sr. To our family he's Dad.

Whether it's a photograph of Dad teaching "the boys," a letter to him from Ben Hogan, a tattered newspaper clipping stuck between the pages to remind us of his 1948 Masters victory, or scorecards attesting to his records—the 61 he shot at both Winged Foot's East and West courses and the 60 at Seminole—the things in our family albums remind us of great days gone by.

(Left to right) Craig Harmon, Dick Harmon, Billy Harmon, and me.

Like our father, all of us are golf professionals—I at Lochinvar in Houston, Craig at Oak Hill Country Club in New York, Dick at Houston's River Oaks C.C., and Billy at the Newport Country Club in Rhode Island. Like our father, too, we are all rated among the top teachers in America. Not a day goes by when we don't think of dear old Dad.

Every single time we give a golf lesson, we're reminded of Dad's teaching philosophy, one that stressed simplicity and the importance of making it fun for the student. That's the kind of deep impression our father left on us.

I know, myself, that when I'm teaching I often feel Dad standing next to me, saying things to remind me of what's important in helping someone learn. Phrases like "Teach adults like you would a second grader," or "The less you say to a student, the more he will learn," or "Don't get so hung up in teaching a pretty golf swing that you forget to teach a student how to feel the clubface and hit the ball" prevent me from confusing my students with overly complex teaching lingo. Rather, they encourage me to provide the student with a singular swing thought that will allow him or her to trigger a technically sound, flowing swing.

And if, for some reason, I can't get a tip across to a student, I take another page out of my father's book and relate the golf swing to another sport or some other action.

For example, if a male player has trouble shifting his weight to the inside portion of his right foot on the backswing, then back to the outside portion of his left foot on the downswing, I first have him visualize a baseball player throwing a pitch. Since most men played ball as kids, this image usually promotes the correct shifting movements of the body. However, if this action has left the player's muscle memory long ago, or he still doesn't "get it," I actually have him pitch balls. During the windup, he feels what golfers should feel during the backswing. During the pitch itself, he feels weight shift to the outside of the left foot just like it does during the golfer's downswing.

To communicate the same message to a female player, I use another one of Dad's tricks: I have her pretend that she's rocking a baby. In a split second she feels what the shifting action is all about.

The thing I like most about my dad's way of teaching is that it is simple and serves everyone. However, he was not a method teacher. He used to tell me time and time again to remember that everyone is different.

"Most people lack strength and flexibility, and either don't have the time to practice or don't like to practice. For this reason, Butch, you need to give them some basic fundamentals and a simple swing that will stand up under the pressure of a club championship or Nassau bet," he told me.

Dad didn't believe in using big words and talking angles like so many of today's teachers. He'd give you the basic movements that you needed, then told you to go on your merry way and learn the nuances common only to you. He was not interested in teaching you how to duplicate a top pro's swing. Regardless of how he respected his fellow professionals, he knew that all but a few were blessed with great flexibility and sheer raw talent.

"Butch, remember this, the average guy on the street can't copy Hogan or Snead's swing," he used to say.

When Dad taught, he talked in layman's language, and geared the swing method to one's personal strengths and natural tendencies. That's why he was so successful. That's why I share some of that success as an instructor.

Something else that shows how my dad was ahead of his time was the way he corrected a bad swing. Whereas his contemporaries would tear apart a faulty action and totally revamp a swing according to the most popular method of the day, Dad would use his keen eye to pinpoint a major fault, then go in there and get rid of it. He didn't worry about the other little things that were wrong with a person's swing. Once he got rid of the "cancer," such as a reverse weight shift, he'd have the student work on his new technique using a short iron, i.e., a 7-iron, 8-iron, 9-iron, or pitching wedge. Each of these clubs is much shorter than a driver, and far less cumbersome to swing while learning to groove a new and better action. What's more, since the correction made to a player's swing was always simple, it took practice minutes, not practice hours, for everything else to fall back into place.

The way my dad communicated ideas to a student helped him get his point across more quickly, so quickly that he rarely finished the half-hour lesson that a student had booked. He'd fix a problem so fast that the student, after hitting a great shot, would look at my father in wonderment.

"Well, go play," my father would say, practically having to kick the student in the butt to get him to leave.

"What about the fifteen minutes we have left, Mr. Harmon?" the student would ask.

My dad's response: "When your doctor diagnoses your problem,

- Do not confuse your student with too much knowledge at once. Pick out the biggest fault and correct that first.

- Do not stereotype your teaching. In other words, do not teach every student the same way. Treat each student as an individual. Each student is different in age, size, strength, and capability. What you teach one student may be the opposite of what you would teach another.

- Make your teaching sessions fun and easy to understand. Create a relaxed atmosphere. The simpler you can explain yourself, the easier it is for your student to comprehend what you are teaching.

- Do not get lazy when you teach. Remember that reassurance and reinforcement are a must. Do not be afraid of constant repetition.

- Pictures do not lie. It is much easier for a student to see his mistakes on film than to hear about them.

- Coach more than teach. Be a cheerleader.

- Most students are poor listeners, so repeat. Stay with the same thought until the student understands you clearly.

- Good teachers diagnose, then prescribe. Concentrate on the student, not on the time of the lesson.

- Use teaching aids whenever possible.

---

then writes you out a prescription, does he hold your hand for another fifteen minutes?"

The student's response: "No."

"Well, neither do I. I figured out your problem and told you how to cure it. Now go take your prescription—in other words, practice!"

For better, or worse, my dad was straight with students. He didn't baby them. He looked at a lesson as an honor and a challenge. He used to say, "Butch, always remember that a person has taken time off from work or given up some leisure time to book a lesson with you. So, no matter how tired or harried you might be, or how bad a player the student is, concentrate hard and find a way to help him or her. If he's tense, tell him a joke to relax him. If she doesn't understand a point you're trying to make, think of an image that will help communicate your instructional message."

This story explains what my father meant when giving me that advice:

Once, on the lesson tee at Winged Foot, a guy was letting his left wrist break down through impact, which in turn caused his right hand to loosen and rotate very quickly over the left hand. This causes the clubface to close and the shot to hook wildly to the left of the target.

To communicate the importance of the left hand staying firm and the right hand going along for the ride (not taking control), my father said this to the student: "You want the left hand to be like Bethlehem Steel; you don't want any linguine coming in there." Two swings later the member was back on track. And there went my dad, walking over to the next person to give him an instant cure.

The time I spend teaching is not the only time I'm reminded of my dad and the legacy he left behind. Every single time I boom a drive down the middle of the fairway, hit a solid iron shot dead to the stick, hit a crisp chip or a soft sand shot, and sink a long putt for par, I think of Dad. After all, the golf games that today belong to me and my brothers once belonged to our dad, our number-one tutor. For that matter, many of the 300-yard drives, crisp iron shots, savvy bunker shots, and solid putts that are being played by members of Seminole, Winged Foot, and Thunderbird Golf Club in Palm Springs (another club my father worked at), can be traced to my father's work on the lesson tee.

I'm fortunate to be from a good golf bloodline. My father, on the other hand, didn't come from a golfing family. His versatile talents were learned the old-fashioned way, through solitary practice, first nurtured in the backyard and schoolyard of his Savannah boyhood neighborhood; then later in Orlando, where he moved while still a youngster.

With a hickory club and a half glove on his left hand, Dad used to spend hours hitting shots out of all kinds of lies. By twilight each day he had invented a half dozen new shots to "put in his bag."

Dad's creative shotmaking prowess is what enabled him to land a job at the prestigious Winged Foot Golf Club, working under Craig Wood, the highly renowned head professional.

Dad was deaf in one ear—an ailment that kept him out of combat and allowed him to work in a Michigan war plant during the 1940s. Fortunately for Dad he was a fine golfer, and the bigwigs used to ask him to join them for regular games. Furthermore, they somehow worked it out so that Dad could work at the plant and still serve as the assistant pro to Ky Laffoon, one of the game's most eccentric golf pros. According to Dad, Laffoon once got so mad at his putter that he attached it to his car with string and let it scrape the ground while he drove to the next tournament; that was his way of punishing his putter. If he really hated a putter, he would drown it in the nearest lake. Although Laffoon was considered to be a bit loony, Dad learned a thing or two about shotmaking from the man his fellow pros called "The Chief."

Around this time, Dad entered a competition at a course in the Chicago area. He was paired with Craig Wood. On one of the holes on the back nine, Dad's ball was sitting in the right rough, 190 yards from the green. The flag was in the front right-hand corner of the green with a big bunker and big oak tree guarding that same side. The situation called for a fade; but at the time, Dad's bread-and-butter shot was a hook.

Dad stood and stared at the situation, finally figuring that if he could hit an enormous 50-yard roping hook shot that started well right of the gaping bunker and tall oak, then hit the back portion of the green, then, just maybe, the ball would follow the slope down to the pin.

According to my dad, Wood was shocked when he saw my father aim 50 yards wide of the green. But, to his surprise, the ball flew solidly off the clubface, started its flight well right of the trouble, continued curving left, hit the green, and rolled down toward the hole.

Wood's response: "Anybody with that much imagination and shot-making talent should work for me."

And for the two of them, it was the start of a very good relationship—with each other and with Winged Foot, where my dad eventually took over for Wood and stayed for 32 years, from 1945 to 1977.

Pros Harry Cooper (*left*) and Craig Wood (*right*) were two of my dad's chief golf mentors.

During this time my father was fortunate enough to be around great players and teachers. He learned a lot from Harry Cooper, Henry Picard, Craig Wood and, of course, Ben Hogan.

Dad also taught Hogan quite a bit about shotmaking, including how to hit the power-cut shot from deep rough with a 4-wood. Previously, Hogan had tried to recover with a long iron and failed, because the long blades of grass grabbed the iron and twisted its face into an open or closed position at impact.

The setup position for playing the power-cut shot from deep rough.

The first time I saw Mr. Hogan hit this shot was at Winged Foot in 1959, when he and Dad were playing together. They had become good friends over the years, and would practice together whenever possible, most of the time at Winged Foot or Seminole. They would play money games to hone their competitive skills and prepare for the pressure of big tournaments. In their matches, Dad beat Hogan as many times as he beat Dad. When I walked along with them at Winged Foot in 1959, it was another serious-friendly match. After all, they were preparing for the U.S. Open championship, which was being played there that year.

During the Open, the United States Golf Association sets the course up to play very fairly. However, if you gamble and don't quite hit the shot as planned, you pay a dear price. This is especially true if one of your tee shots strays into the rough bordering the fairway. In U.S. Opens, the rough is allowed to grow very high, which is troublesome for a couple of reasons, the most obvious one being that it's very difficult to recover with a low-lofted iron. The less obvious reason is that, if you do happen to make solid contact, you have to worry about hitting a *flyer,* a shot that flies extra fast off the clubface, then carries 10 to 20 yards farther than a normal shot hit with the same club. How far the ball flies depends on how much grass intervenes between the ball and the clubface at impact. (Grass has moisture in it. The more blades of grass that intervene, the more moisture. The more moisture, the more the grooves on the clubface lose their grip on the ball. Consequently, it's nearly impossible to impart backspin on the ball, resulting in a longer shot than normal.)

In order to hit a solid shot out of heavy rough, and hold one of the fast-running, sloping greens at Winged Foot's West Course (or at any course with similar features), you have to hit a super-cut with a 4-wood. The one that Dad taught Hogan can be used between 150 and 180 yards out from the green.

To play this shot, assume an exaggerated open alignment by aiming your feet, knees, hips, and shoulders as much as 50 yards left of the target. That's open! Make sure to point the toe end of your left foot outward

In playing the power-cut, allow your right wrist to hinge early in the takeaway, to help you swing the club up on a steep plane (*left*); then, as you start down, push down on your left foot to help you accelerate the club at a faster speed, and swing the club on an even steeper plane (*right*).

more than normal, as this promotes a brisker and freer clearing action of the left hip on the downswing. Ultimately, this swing action will earn you the power you're seeking. The ball should be played off your left heel, with your hands even with the ball or slightly behind it. Set the club down behind the ball with its face wide open.

On the backswing, swing the club almost straight up into the air, on a very steep plane. Coming down, "just beat on it," as Dad told Ben. The wood will act like a sickle and cut through the deep rough, sending the ball flying far down the fairway with a left-to-right flight. The fade pattern of the shot will allow it to land softly on the green.

The address position for playing the super-long bunker shot.

This shot can also be hit with a 5- or 6-wood. Don't be afraid to use it at your own club, during a championship, when the greenskeeper leaves the rough long.

Many of the shots my dad learned he taught himself in an effort to deal with the challenging conditions at Winged Foot and Seminole. Because both of these courses feature plateau-type greens that are two-tiered, undulating, and surrounded by big bunkers and testy rough, Dad's inventiveness was geared more to the short game. In fact, many golf experts still rank him the best bunker player who ever lived.

I must admit, I've had the pleasure of seeing some great bunker players during my life: Julius Boros, Gary Player, Sam Snead, Seve Ballesteros, and Greg Norman are just a few. But I have to tell you, I wouldn't dispute the opinions of the golf experts. Make no mistake, Dad was the greatest out of sand, particularly when playing extra-long bunker shots.

Here's a shot he invented one day when hitting out of a bunker situated about 50 yards from Winged Foot's 9th green. Seventy-five yards was his total distance to the hole. Use it when you find yourself in a similar situation.

Because the shot was so long, Dad knew he couldn't hit a normal explosion shot with a sand wedge and expect to reach the green, let alone the hole. He figured he could try to pick the ball clean off the surface of the sand with a pitching wedge, but that was always risky; nine out of ten times you mishit the ball—certainly not a high percentage shot.

In telling me the story of how he invented this shot, Dad told me he

The super-long sand shot technique: impact, follow-through.

Dad's expertise was hardly limited to specialty shots. Here is his explanation of the basic fundamentals of the golf swing:

The backswing is initiated by the left shoulder moving to the right of the ball. At the waist-high position the clubshaft should be parallel to the target line. The toe of the club pointing straight up signals a "square" position. At this point in the swing, the upper part of your left arm should remain against the side of your chest. I believe it is essential to maintain the right leg posture and feel some tension from your right foot into your right leg. Your head and the spine should move behind the ball on the backswing. Your weight should go in the direction the club is traveling.

At the top of the swing, the position of the clubface should be somewhere near a square position. Square, to me, is a position of the clubface that is parallel to the position of the left forearm. Your left shoulder should be over the inside of your right knee. Approximately 75 percent of your weight should be on your right leg. Your shoulders will be turned approximately 90 degrees and your hips approximately 40 degrees.

The downswing starts from the ground up. Initiate the downswing with the transfer of weight to your left leg. Your body will begin to rotate to the left. Let the unwinding of the body bring your arms and hands down. Do not start the downswing by trying to hit with your right hand. Your legs, hips, and stomach muscles rotate and move the club through to impact. Never try to rush the transition from the backswing to the downswing. You must try to maintain a smooth rhythmic tempo.

The best way to describe what to do on the downswing is to try to turn through and face the target. The one common denominator in the golf swing is that no matter what type of backswing is used by good players, they all arrive at impact with the left wrist flat and the clubface dead square to the target.

---

stared down at the ball, then back up at the bunker a few times, trying to think the shot through logically, with the same intensity Sherlock Holmes would exhibit when solving a murder.

Five minutes later he concluded that if he opened the clubface of a 6-iron, played the ball off his left heel, assumed an open stance, used his normal bunker shot swing, and delivered the club into a spot about an inch behind the ball, the shot would fly high enough to carry the lip, but low enough to land deeper into the green. He swung. The ball flew low as planned, bounced once near the hole, then stopped dead.

Greg Norman and Seve Ballesteros both play a similar shot to Dad's, only with an 8- or 9-iron. So don't be afraid to experiment. Maybe you can hit an even better shot with a 5-iron.

Dad's creativity extended well into the area of the short game. He was a particularly inventive chipper, and I recommend you add the following two specialty shots to your repertoire, as I did years ago, if you want to improve your short game.

The first of these shots should be used when facing an extremely long chip off fringe grass (something in the 100-foot range) to a hole situated at the back of a fast-running green. Many golfers who face this shot

The advantage of playing a long chip with a long iron is this: Once you assume an open address position (*left*), all you need to do is stay locked into that address while making an extrashort backswing (*middle*), then an equally short downswing action, with your right knee turning inward (*right*).

Because the club features a low degree of loft, all you need is a short swing to send the ball rolling all the way to the hole, like a putt.

usually play a putter, or try to pitch the ball all the way to the cup. Both of these are poor options.

To reach the hole with a putter, you have to swing harder. Right there is a red flag; how hard to swing is a question you can't answer because you're not used to hitting a putt this long off the fringe. Also, because you're not used to swinging the putter at a higher speed, you have no idea how far you will hit the ball; you're guessing, which is something no good golfer does.

Hitting the shot with the pitching wedge is no percentage play either. Unless you've practiced this shot a thousand times, it will be very difficult for you to hit the ball softly into the air so precisely that it lands by the pin, then stops. If you don't put enough oomph into the shot, the

The 3-wood chip: the address.

ball will finish well short of the hole. Hit the ball too hard and you'll send it flying over the green, probably into a sand trap or some other trouble spot.

The shot to play here is one my dad invented—the running chip with a 3-iron. This club is so good in this situation because it allows you to make an even shorter and slower stroke than normal. Therefore, you have much more control over the shot. Take a look at the accompanying photographs of me playing this chip shot and you'll see what I mean by "shorter stroke." I swing the club back just past my right shoe. And my follow-through stops just past impact.

Try this shot. The ball carries the fringe grass, lands on the green, and rolls all the way back to the hole.

Tailoring the Tip: You low-handicap players, with good feel for the clubhead, should try this shot if the ball sits on the green about 75 to 100 feet from the hole. You'll find that, because you can impart a little spin on the ball, it's much easier to judge than a putt.

One of the most inventive short-game shots that Dad taught me 35 years ago, and one a few Tour players use today to handle the heavy fringe grass, is a chip—believe it or not—with a 3-wood.

If you face a funky lie in the fringe—ball down slightly, high grass behind it—the natural thing is to reach for either a pitching wedge, sand wedge, or third wedge. In this situation, none of these clubs will work. The natural tendency is to swing the wedge back on a very upright angle, thus coming down sharply into the ball. When grass is behind the ball and you use a steep swing, you will inevitably hit an uncontrollable flyer that runs well past the hole.

The next time you face this situation, leave the wedge in your bag

The 3-wood chip: the backswing, the downswing.

and play a 3-wood using this technique: play the ball in the middle of an open stance, so that your hands are level with the ball. In taking the club back and through, promote a more level swing by keeping the wrists calm and controlling the action with your arms and shoulders, just as you do when putting. Notice how the club's shape allows it to glide through the grass and make clean contact with the ball. The 14 or 15 degrees of loft built into the face of the 3-wood will send the ball flying softly over the heavy fringe grass in front of you, then roll it quietly to the hole.

Just in case you're like the hundreds of busy businessmen on the run who confessed to my dad that they had no time to practice, or hated it, let me tear a page out of my father's lesson book and give you a variety of quick tips for learning a specific element of the swing, or playing different long and short shots.

Harmon's Hints, or Just Do It!

Hit Through the Hula Hoop.

If you become nervous when staring down a tree-lined fairway, often making a bad swing and mishitting the shot, change your "outlook." Imagine a big hula hoop about five feet in front of you that you are going to hit the ball through. This task is a heck of a lot simpler than focusing on a target some 220 yards down the fairway. For this reason, you'll be super-relaxed when you look back down at the ball, make a good swing and, coincidentally, hit your distant target.

How High to Tee the Ball When Driving.

To promote powerfully hit, accurate shots, tee up so that half of the ball is above the top of the clubface. Just do it, and you'll hit the ball squarely on the upswing.

The Power Sweep.

To build your golf muscles and strengthen your body turn, practice swinging with a heavy broom. Because this is heavier and longer than the average driver, you'll feel like Superman when you put a lightweight metal driver back in your hand. Consequently, you'll generate high club-head speed and hit longer tee shots.

The Power Stretch.

Grip the club cross-handed. Because your left hand is lower than your right, you'll get a better feel for the stretching of the left side of your body during a power swing.

Revert to your normal grip and swing. Watch the ball fly fast off the clubface and far down the fairway.

Hit the Forward Ball.

If you're not hitting the ball as far as you should with your fairway woods, you're probably not accelerating the club through the impact zone. To promote a powerful follow-through, imagine a second ball a couple of inches in front of the one you will actually hit. Try to hit that second ball and you'll hit the "real" one more powerfully than ever before.

Senior Savvy.

You senior players with limited strength and flexibility can increase your turning power, clubhead speed, and driving distance by letting your left heel lift and wrists hinge sooner on the backswing.

How To Hit a 1-Iron.

The best way to learn how to hit a 1-iron is to first realize that it features about seven more degrees of loft than the average driver.

Tee up about 12 balls and hit the first 6 with a 5-iron. Then hit the remaining balls with your 1-iron, pretending it is a 5-iron. Now you'll be less apt to "force" the 1-iron on the course and make a mess of things scorewise.

Higher Ground.

In playing long-iron or fairway wood shots off hilly fairway lies, always play the ball closer to the higher foot. In other words, on downhill lies, closer to your right foot; on uphill lies, closer to your left foot.

What to Do When the Ball Is Below Your Feet.

Bend more at the knees. Toe the clubface in slightly to compensate for exaggerated left-to-right flight.

What to Do When the Ball Is Above Your Feet.

Choke down on the grip. Toe the clubface out slightly to compensate for exaggerated right-to-left flight.

How to Hit Strong Long Irons.

Promote a full backswing turn by turning your left shoulder over your right knee. Promote a powerful hit and fluid follow-through by turning your right shoulder under your chin.

How to Cheat the Wind.

Take one more club for the required distance (e.g., a 6-iron instead of a 7-iron), and swing more smoothly. The ball will fly lower because you used a less lofted club, and it will fly with more control because you swung more slowly.

What to Do When the Fairway Is Wet.

Take one more club than you would normally hit from the same distance. This will promote a smoother, more compact swing. Furthermore, it will allow you to sweep the ball—not dig the club into the soft, wet turf.

Confidence Trick.

Here's a little trick that will help you hit a solid shot off a tight fairway lie:

If you think you can hit the shot with a 3-wood, select a more lofted 4-wood. Giving yourself that one-club safety margin will give you the confidence you need to execute this tough shot.

Crosswind Strategies.

When playing in a crosswind, follow these rules:

1. On tee shots, let the ball ride the wind. For example, if a strong wind is blowing from right to left, aim right and let the wind carry the ball back into the center of the fairway.

2. On approach shots into the green, turn the ball into the wind. In a left-to-right wind, hit a draw.

That Nerve-Racking 40-Yard Pitch.

The most common faults amateurs have when hitting this shot are a long backswing and letting the club decelerate through impact. Don't you make the same mistakes. When facing this type of pitch shot, make a compact backswing and hit through with authority.

Chipping to a Wet Green.

In this situation, simply select a stronger, less lofted club than your favorite 7-iron. The decreased loft will cause the ball to fly lower and roll faster toward the hole.

Putting on Wet Greens.

Allow for about half as much break.

Putting Downhill on Fast Greens.

In this situation, strike the ball with the lighter toe end of the putterhead to deaden the hit.

Putting on Slow Greens.

On very slow greens, move the ball forward in your stance. This will encourage you to hit the top portion of the ball and impart overspin to it.

How to Handle Severe Uphill Putts.

To encourage yourself to reach the hole, pretend that the hole is about five feet farther away.

How to Handle Severe Downhill Putts.

To guard against hitting the ball too far past the hole, pretend that it is closer to you. The steeper the slope, the closer you should imagine the hole.

What to Do When the Green Slopes Severely From Left to Right.

Play the ball off your left instep to ensure that the putterface hits the ball as the face is almost closing. This strategy is a good one because it virtually guarantees that you keep the ball on the "high" side of the hole.

What to Do When the Green Slopes Severely From Right to Left.

Play the ball off your right instep to ensure that the putterface remains open and that you keep the ball on the "pro" side of the hole.

Green Reading.

On very tricky greens only, read the putt from four angles: from behind the ball, from behind the hole, from the left side, and from the right side.

Putting With the Grain.

When the blades of grass along the target line lean toward the hole, there will be a sheen to the grass. This means that the speed of the putt will increase. Allow for this by making a slightly slower stroke.

Putting Into the Grain.

When the blades of grass along the ball-hole line run toward you, there will be a dullness to the green. In this situation, hit the ball more firmly.

Chipping From Sand.

If the lie is good, the bunker's lip is low, and you have ample green to work with, you can chip instead of exploding.

Play the ball back in your stance with your hands ahead of it. Now just make a pure pendulum stroke, allowing the big muscles of your arms and shoulders to control the action.

Be a Studious Chipper.

Before chipping, study the line and breaks on the green, just as you would when getting ready to putt.

What to Do When Playing an Uphill Chip.

The steeper the slope, the less lofted club you should play.

What to Do When Playing a Downhill Chip.

The steeper the slope, the more lofted club you should play.

Hardpan Recovery.

In playing a long iron off hardpan, close the clubface slightly at address; the clubface is likely to open at impact, once it hits the hard ground.

The Water Shot.

My father played this shot from a water hazard on the 15th hole of the final round, en route to winning the 1948 Masters.

Yes, you too can play this greenside shot, provided at least half of the ball is above the surface of the water. My father used a sand wedge to recover. I suggest you play a 60-degree wedge, a club that wasn't around when Dad won the Masters. This club features less bounce and will therefore cut through the water more easily. Furthermore, its added loft will help you hit a floating shot that gets up quickly and lands extra softly. Here are my father's three simple swing secrets for this shot:

1. Hold the club above the water, with its face open.
2. Swing the club up on a very steep angle.
3. Hit down sharply, into a spot directly behind the ball.

Stay Loose When the Ball Is Tight Against the Collar.

When the ball is dead against the fringe's collar, don't panic, as many amateurs do. Don't use a putter either, which is another common error made by the club-level player. Play a wedge and use this technique:

Line up the clubhead's leading edge, or "blade," with the equator of the ball. Employ a firm-wristed putting stroke, hitting the ball where it rises above the long grass.

Because of the wedge's generous heavy flange, you'll hit the ball nice and solid, rolling it to the hole like a putt.

L-Wedge Off Tight Fairways.

If you're a sand-wedge distance from the flag, but on a firm part of the fairway, switch to a more lofted L-wedge. The L-wedge's sharper leading edge and limited bounce area will help you dig down into the extra-firm, dried-out turf.

The lob wedge is more lofted than the sand wedge. Therefore, the ball will fly higher and not as far. Make a fuller swing to make up for the loss in yardage.

Tee Up on Par-Three Holes.

Don't play your tee shots off the grass on par-three holes. Tee up the ball.

A tee raises your level of confidence. Furthermore, it eliminates the risk of hitting a "flyer" over the green.

Ball Perched Up High in Rough.

This is an easy shot to pop up. So promote a sweeping hit by taking one more club, aligning the sole of the club with the bottom of the ball, and controlling the swing with your arms.

Ball on Pine Needles.

Before concentrating on swing technique, hold the clubhead slightly above the needles, so as to not dislodge the ball and cost yourself a penalty stroke. Also, carefully clear the patches of pine needles under your feet to secure your footing (if you think you can without causing the ball to move).

When you're ready to swing, keep the backswing action compact, then use your hands and arms to lead the club directly into the back of the ball.

Ball in Scottish Heather.

If you happen to travel to the birthplace of golf, you're bound to have to play at least one shot from heather—a wiry purple-flowered plant that's notorious for grabbing the neck of your club and twisting the face closed.

To recover, assume an open alignment, with the ball well back in your stance, and 70 percent of your weight on your left foot.

Take the club up steeply.

Pull the club down hard.

One more thing: if you're facing a greenside shot from heather, take a pitching wedge instead of a sand wedge; its sharper leading edge will help you slice through the thick stuff.

How to Handle Clover.

The ball will fly at least ten yards farther out of clover than out of normal fairway grass. The moisture in the clover leaves intervenes between the ball and clubface at impact. Compensate for this by taking a weaker, more lofted club.

The Texas Wedge Shot.

When the fairway grass fronting the green is cut fairly low, there's no reason to chip. Instead, use this technique to play the "Texas wedge" shot with a putter:

Play the ball a little farther back in your stance than you would normally when putting.

Make your normal stroke; however, swing a trifle harder to allow for the fairway grass slowing down the speed of the putt.

Half-Sand, Half-Grass Lie.

From this greenside lie, lay the clubface open at address.

Swing the club up quickly, allowing your wrists to hinge freely.

Hit down more firmly than if you were playing a normal sand shot from the same distance.

Ball Under Bush, Normal Swing Impeded.

Kneel, planting the knees wide apart. Aim right to allow for hook.

Swing the club back and through with your arms.

Ball in Ice Plant.

You'll run into this lie if you visit courses on the West Coast.

To recover from ice plant around the green, open your stance and put 70 percent of your weight on your left foot.

Use a steep swing, hitting the ball first.

How to Play a Middle Iron from Deep Rough.

Play the ball back in your stance, with your hands a couple of inches ahead of it. Open the clubface.

Swing the club back on an exaggerated upright plane, allowing your wrists to cock quickly.

On the downswing, pull the club down hard, smacking the back center portion of the ball with the sweet spot of the clubface.

Go With "Your" Shot.

To be a smart course strategist and shoot low scores, you must play "your" shot whenever possible.

To determine your most common ball flight, hit 25 shots with a 5-iron from a square stance. The shot you hit most, a fade or draw, is your bread-and-butter shot.

Over a Bank, Toward the Cup.

Here's how to play an extra-high shot when your ball flies the green and comes to rest at the base of a steep bank.

Play the ball off your left instep and put 60 percent of your weight on your right foot. Open the clubface.

Swing the club on an upright backswing plane.

On the downswing, bring the club down and through to a high finish, while keeping your head behind the ball.

Extrasoft Pitch to a Hard Green.

Open the clubface of a lofted wedge, swing the club back outside the target line, swing across the ball coming through.

Bank On It.

To hit the ball into a grassy bank so that it bounces up, then rolls gently to the hole, play the ball back in your stance. Keep your head perfectly still, and most of your weight on your left side, while making a dead-wristed arm swing.

Mini-Pitch From Grassy Lie.

Use a wristy bunker-type swing and hit two inches behind the ball with your sand wedge, as if you were trying to purposely hit a fat shot.

Low Shot Under Branches.

To hit a greenside shot under overhanging branches, select a low-lofted club. Keep the lower body quiet while swinging the club back and through fluidly, with your arms controlling the action.

Chipping to Tight Pin on Fast Green.

Swing the club back normally. Turn your right hand under your left through impact; this turning-under action allows you to put the full loft of the clubface under the ball. The ball will land more softly, then trickle to the hole.

Alternative Method: Swing back normally. On the downswing, concentrate on pushing the back of your left hand downward, toward the ground. Watch the ball pop out softly.

Quick Draw.

If you need to hit a big draw around trees, aim your body to the right of the target—where you want the ball to start its flight. Aim the clubface at your final target—where you want the ball to end its flight.

Swing normally. The ball will fly to the right of the trees, then curve sharply left toward the green.

Be a Heel.

To promote an outside-in swing path and a fade shot off the tee, play the ball closer to the heel of the driverface.

Holeouts.

The most important swing keys for recovering from a divot hole are keeping the hands well ahead of the ball at address and keeping the hands well ahead of the clubhead through impact.

How to Hit a High Iron Shot.

Set up with the ball off your left instep and most of your weight on your right foot.

How to Hit a Low Iron Shot.

Set up with the ball just behind the midpoint in your stance and most of your weight on your left foot.

What to Do If Your Iron Shots Lack Power.

Promote the strongest possible turn on the backswing by rotating your left shoulder over your right knee.

Once you're wound up to the max, encourage the strongest possible hit by unwinding from the ground up.

What to Do If You're Confused About Ball Position.

If you're new to the game, you probably don't know whether to play every shot off your left heel, opposite your left armpit, or to move the ball back progressively as the clubs increase in loft.

The best way to figure out "your" ball position is to swing a club and note where it touches the grass. Make a few swings. The spot in the grass where you've worn it thin is the spot to play that particular iron club.

Go through your entire bag and for each club, figure out where the best place to position the ball is.

Do Your Tee Shots Skip?

If your tee shots hit the ground before rising into the air, you've got a downswing problem. Here's how to cure it.

Keep your upper body and head behind the ball through impact. Staying back allows the arms to extend while the club sweeps the ball cleanly off the tee on a level path.

What to Do If You Take the Club Back Outside the Target Line and Slice.

When setting up, be sure that your right arm is slightly lower than your left. Dipping your right shoulder slightly will help you assume the correct address position. This one simple setup adjustment will allow you to swing the club on the correct inside-square-inside path and hit accurate shots.

Is It Okay to Be Unorthodox?

If you putt successfully with the heel or the toe of the putter off the ground, don't change your action to match that of your favorite pro. Putting is the most individualistic aspect of golf. Don't worry about what others think about your unique style. Do your thing—if it works!

Cure for Swaying.

If your body sways and you mishit shots, set up with your right knee flexed more and pointed slightly inward. Keep that position throughout the backswing.

Is Your Backswing Too Short?

If you answered yes to this question, allow your left heel to lift off the ground.

What to Do When the Sand Is Powdery.

Sand that's of a powdery texture is less resistant to the wedge. Therefore, you must hit farther behind the ball.

What to Do When the Sand Is Coarse.

Deliver the clubhead into a spot closer behind the ball than you would normally.

Lucky Bounces.

When selecting a sand wedge, pick one that features a "bounce" that's suited to the texture of sand in your bunkers. For example, if the sand at your course is firm, buy a wedge with a limited bounce and a sharp leading edge. If the sand is soft, buy a wedge with a big bounce.

Cure for Hitting Chips Left of the Hole.

If you pull chips well left of the hole, play the ball back farther in your stance, and swing the club on a more inside path.

Cure for Hitting Chips Right of the Hole.

If you push chips well right of the hole, play the ball more forward in your stance, and swing the club on a less inside path.

What to Do If You Open the Clubface at Impact and Push Putts.

If this happens to you when putting, you're probably crowding the ball; try standing slightly farther away from it.

Missing Short Putts?

You're probably looking up, or "peeking," before impact.

Next time you putt, wait to listen for the ball to clang the metal cup before looking up.

Freezing Over the Ball.

Use a forward press action to trigger the swing. For example, rotate your right knee inward, then start your swing.

Confidence Booster.

The next time you panic on the first tee, recall a powerfully hit accurate drive you once made. That mental image will allow you to make a tension-free, technically sound swing.

What to Do When You're Down in a Match.

Forget about what your opponent is doing. Play the course. Concentrate on hitting fairways and greens.

Swing Rehearsal.

If you're one of those golfers who tense up in sand, test your swing out in the grass outside the bunker. That way, when you step into the trap, you'll be confident and perform like a pro.

Wet Weather Golf.

Always carry at least one extra glove and a spare towel in your golf bag, just in case it rains.

Keep the Same Mind-set.

You'll find you'll shoot a lower total score if you don't get overexcited by either a birdie or a bogey.

What to Do When Putting in Wind.

Widen your stance a few inches and put more weight on your left foot to establish a firm foundation for your stroke.

Know Your Course Like a Book.

To give yourself the best possible chance of shooting a low score on your home course, you must know it. So, before the club championship, put together a little notebook, noting trees, traps, water hazards, yardages to landing areas, and common pin placements.

Stand Tall on Long Putts.

If you use too much wrist action and mishit long putts, remedy your problem by standing taller to the ball. By not bending as much from the knees, you will encourage a pendulum stroke, controlled mainly with the arms.

Check Your Clubs.

Check your grips from time to time. If grime builds up on a grip, the club will slip in your hands, causing you to mishit the ball. Wash your grips with soapy water and towel dry. If you can't put "life" back into the grips, buy new ones.

How to Hit a Super Lag Putt.

Imagine a washtub, three feet in diameter, with a flagstick in the middle of it. Hit the ball into the tub and you've hit a great lag putt.

How to Hit Short Fairway Bunker Shots.

Wriggle your feet into the sand slightly to establish a firm foundation for swinging the club smoothly through the ball. Don't dig your feet too deeply into the sand. Otherwise, you'll chop down.

Standing taller will also encourage you to pick the ball cleanly off the sand and hit a more solid shot.

Where's the "Sweet Spot" on Your Putter?

If there's no dot, arrow, or other kind of marker indicating the sweet spot of your putter, hold it by the grip end with your left thumb and forefinger, so that it suspends vertically in the air. Tap the putterface at different spots with a coin. When you find a spot that causes the putter to swing straight back without wobbling, you've discovered the sweet spot. Now mark it with paint.

Steady Now.

You'll make a more consistently good stroke and hit more on-line putts if you keep your head perfectly still on the backswing and downswing. Don't watch the putterhead as it swings back and through.

Backyard Practice.

Lay four clubs on your backyard lawn so that they form a rectangular box. Then practice lofting shots into that area with a variety of wedges.

Palms Parallel.

Whether you use a weak, neutral, or strong grip, make sure that your palms are parallel to each other.

Regain the Feel for the Release.

If you feel that your downswing release action is inhibited, try this drill:

Hold the club just above the ball.

Make a few practice swings.

Almost immediately, you'll feel how the arms, wrists, and hands should work as a team to whip the club into the ball.

Use Your Imagination.

In lining up a breaking putt, imagine a second ball at a point where you think the ball you're going to hit will start curving. Hit that imaginary ball and you'll hole out.

Post-Round Practice.

Instead of going home disgusted after a bad round, go to the practice tee and work only with those clubs that gave you a problem on the course.

A Small Wager Will Help You Handle Pressure.

To get accustomed to putting under pressure, play an 18-hole match against a friend or fellow club member, and "put something on it."

How to Flatten an Overly Steep Plane.

Tall players sometimes fall into the bad habit of swinging the club back on an overly steep angle. To remedy this fault, think of turning your shoulders in a clockwise direction and swinging your left arm across your chest.

C u r e   f o r   a   R e v e r s e   P i v o t .

If you rock your weight left on the backswing, leave it on the right side on the downswing, and hit weak shots, you're probably moving your head toward the target on the backswing. To cure this problem, turn your left shoulder behind the ball.

On the

CHAPTER FOUR

Lesson Tee

WHAT I TAUGHT GREG NORMAN,

DAVIS LOVE III, AND

U.S. AMATEUR CHAMPION TIGER WOODS

CAN HELP YOU BREAK

YOUR SCORING BARRIER

Golf is a fascinating game in so many ways, but to me one of its most interesting aspects is the fact that it is played by so many different levels of players. These levels range from the weekend amateur all the way up to superstar athletes like Greg Norman, Nick Price, and Nick Faldo. I'm not sure the public realizes just what fine golfers these guys are, unless they have watched them in person, seen how purely and powerfully they strike the ball on the practice tee, and observed how well they score on championship course setups that would cause the everyday amateur to shoot 20 strokes higher than average. These players are to golf what Michael Jordan is to basketball, Joe Montana to football, Mickey Mantle to baseball.

On the other side of the coin, there are millions of golfers who, let's face it, play the game very poorly. Their mechanics are very bad, they miss many more shots than they hit well, their mental approach to the game is haphazard, and they never break 100. Yet, like the Normans, Prices, and Faldos, they really love golf and they want to get better.

What unites all golfers I've met who have played the game for a while and are hooked on it is that no matter what level they play the game at, they want to improve. Even when Greg Norman or Nick Price or Nick Faldo wins the British Open one week (and they all have), I guarantee you that the next week they are going to be hitting balls, chipping and putting, consulting with their teachers, and plotting to figure out what adjustments they can make that will help them score even better in the next tournament. To their way of thinking, they have not yet mastered the game and they never will. They are not so good that they can't improve. And, quite frankly, they are absolutely right.

Greg Norman has had a tremendous reputation since he first came to America in the early 1980s as a superstar player. He was quickly dubbed "The Great White Shark" because of his white-blonde hair, his exploits during shark fishing expeditions, and his competitive, attacking nature on the golf course. Of course, Greg hit the ball very long, got into contention in a lot of major tournaments, and quickly became not only a crowd favorite but a favorite in every tournament he entered.

Over the years from about 1982 through 1990, Greg played some tremendous golf, finishing as the PGA Tour's leading money winner in 1986 and in 1990. Yet, somehow, his record (at least in the U.S.) did not quite match the massive expectations set for him. During the 1982–90 period, he won a bank full of money, but he only won nine PGA Tour events and one major title, the 1986 British Open. Of course, much has been made about the fact that Greg Norman has had one of the most unlucky careers anyone can remember, in which opponent after opponent pulled off shocking wins against him. There was the 1984 U.S. Open playoff loss to Fuzzy Zoeller. There was a star-crossed 1986, when Jack Nicklaus caught lightning in a bottle on the last nine at the Masters, while Norman floundered to a bogey on the 18th, fouling up just enough to hand Jack the title. Then at that year's PGA, Bob Tway's holed sand shot on the 72nd hole did Greg in after he led virtually all the way. In 1987, it was Larry Mize's miracle 140-foot chip-in to take the Masters in a playoff. The list of fabled Norman losses is seemingly endless.

I agree to some extent with the popular opinion that Norman has lost a lot of heartbreakers. However, I must add another point that might sound surprising and critical, but one with which I believe Greg Norman would be the first to agree. That is, Greg's swing during those years was not very sound, and it was this unsoundness that was the real cause of all those eleventh-hour losses. If Greg had been able to execute under extreme pressure as he should have, he would have locked the door on those guys who wound up beating him.

I realize that you might be saying to yourself: wait a minute, how can you say Greg Norman's mechanics weren't that sound? How can anyone's mechanics not be sound if he is winning millions of dollars and is in contention all the time?

Let me answer that by recalling a little bit of history, going back as far as 1984. At the U.S. Open that year, at Winged Foot, Norman was playing the 18th hole tied with Zoeller, who was playing right behind him. On this tough par-four finisher, from the middle of the fairway, Greg hit a middle iron that had to be one of the wildest pushes to the right that anyone in that situation has ever hit. The ball went straight into the gallery stands on that side of the green. From there, all Greg could do was get the ball back on the green, at least 40 feet from the hole. Amazingly, he made the putt and forced a playoff. But it's reasonable to ask, why didn't Greg hit the green in regulation? Then that 40-footer would have won it outright instead of putting him in a playoff, which wound up being a Zoeller blowout.

In 1986 at the Masters: Nicklaus shot a first-round 65 while the crowd went absolutely crazy and visions of a sixth title for the Golden Bear loomed. Still, Norman was in the 18th fairway, needing birdie to win, par to tie. Instead, he launched another 4-iron into the gallery to the right. From that position, there was no way to get it up and down, and Jack headed for Butler Cabin to try on another green jacket.

The key point is that Greg was always fighting what is often the "good player's bad shot"—the shot that flies straight and far, but well to the right of the target. And the stronger the player and the longer he hits the ball, the bigger this problem becomes.

At any rate, in 1991 Norman had his second-worst year ever, finishing 53rd on the PGA Tour money list. Those in the know were whispering that Greg was finished as a top player, that the psychological effects of all those tough losses had piled up and finally overcome him. Plus, since he was getting close to age 40, it was probably too late for him to come back.

Those theories were and are, quite frankly, a bunch of baloney. Greg Norman not only became as good as he ever was, he became a lot better, by changing his setup and swing mechanics. Greg came to me at the end of that 1991 season and we looked at a lot of film and videotapes, then went about rebuilding first his long game, then his pitching game. Later, we worked on his putting. By studying the adjustments I made with Greg, you, too, can learn how to improve your game.

The Setup

To most observers, Greg's setup position in 1990 would look pretty good. But there was one significant flaw that was hurting him—his stance was a little too narrow. So the most significant setup adjustment we implemented was for Greg to widen his stance by moving his right foot a few inches farther to the right. This key adjustment gave him a firm foundation and, as we'll see, improved his balance as he swung the club up to the top.

Although it's difficult to detect when you watch Greg play on television or at a tournament, his weight is balanced 50/50 on both feet. In the past, in his driver setup, he would have a tendency to leave too much weight on his right foot, which again made it easier to slide onto the outside of his right foot at the top. The ultimate shotmaking result: a block hit well right of target.

I also adjusted Greg's hands and arms at address slightly. In the old setup, Greg tended to let his hands get a touch behind the ball with the driver. When a player's hands get behind the ball at address, he or she will usually take the club back from the ball outside the target line. This, of course, contributes to a cutting action through impact. I asked Greg to move his left hand forward an inch, no more than two, toward the target.

Greg Norman's old setup shows how he used to set his hands behind the ball.

This position promotes a nice takeaway path, starting straight back and then moving gradually inside the target line as the shoulders turn. Also, Greg reduced the degree of tightness with which he gripped the club. If you remember, in Chapter Two I stated that you should hold the club moderately firmly, but that the stronger you are, the lighter your hold on

In Greg's new setup, his left hand is ahead of, not behind, the ball.

the club will probably feel. Well, Greg is a very strong guy and he was holding the club on the tight side even for him. By relaxing the tension in his hands and arms slightly, he found he could make a freer swing and generate even more clubhead speed. Make sure that you're not strangling the club, either. You'll soon begin to notice the effect it has on your swing.

Tightening Up the Swinging Action

Once I got these setup adjustments into place, Greg's swing adjustments followed relatively easily. Let's discuss the old flaws first.

In attempting to hit the ball long (and believe me, Greg still tries to hit it long—but he does so with his body under control), Greg's weight

Greg's old swing was much too long.

would shift onto the outside of his right foot. He was always on the brink of losing his balance at the top. You might say he was always teetering near the red line in terms of his body control with the driver.

Let's take a look at Norman's old position at the top of the backswing. Notice how the clubshaft has moved beyond parallel to the ground, and the wrists look a little loose or "flippy." This is a direct consequence of his old setup. Because Greg's stance was narrow, he picked the club up into a steep backswing arc. Whenever you pick the club up fairly abruptly, there is a tendency for the wrists to cock much more at the top of the backswing. This cocking is not all bad; most players need some wrist cock at the top in order to generate power. However, when the club is dropping below parallel because of excessive wrist cock, a player's timing has to be perfect because the clubface simply is not under as much control. In Greg's case, he would get away with this most days— but getting away with it most days wasn't good enough on the 72nd hole of a major.

During Greg's slump, he got more and more into the habit of triggering his downswing by driving his legs very hard. He drove the legs so hard that, with the driver, his right foot would actually get pulled off the ground and toward the target. Greg's weight was definitely getting outside the boundaries of staying in balance, both on the backswing and the downswing. Because of this hard leg slide toward the target, Norman periodically would get ahead of the ball, leaving the clubface open and thus pushing the ball to the right. The greater the pressure, the more the club would lag behind him on the downswing, and the bigger the "block" that would follow.

But look closely at the illustration of Greg's backswing today. Notice how much more compact it is. With the new, wider stance there are two immediate benefits: Greg is able to take the club back lower to the ground, creating the widest arc possible. His right leg is much better braced against the movement of his weight to the right. It's positioned as solidly as a rock. Now look at how much firmer Greg's hands and wrists look at the top. He has made just as much of a shoulder turn as ever, yet the clubshaft is slightly short of parallel to the ground rather than beyond parallel. In sum, Greg is in a perfect position to deliver the club with controlled power on the downswing.

If, after making these adjustments, your backswing plane is too steep, you can cure your fault quickly and groove a flatter swing by hitting iron shots off a lie that is above your feet. This is how I helped Greg; and, if I say so myself, he's never looked back.

Even though Greg's new swing is shorter, his arc is wide and powerful.

In Greg's downswing, only one adjustment was needed, given the virtually perfect setup and backswing positions he had attained. This was to eliminate his tendency to drive his legs too hard toward the target. I worked on getting Greg to feel that the downswing was initiated by his left hip, rather than his legs. I asked Greg to think "bump and turn," making the initial move with the left hip toward the target, then rotating it counterclockwise. This rotational element is what really made Greg's downswing plane flatter, or shallower, than in the past; he didn't do it by manipulating his hands and arms differently. This shallower plane allowed him to sweep the ball off the ground or the tee for the most solid possible hit.

One minor problem in the downswing that Greg needed to solve was his habit of letting his right foot be pulled forward off the ground through the impact zone—a by-product of that overzealous leg action. Here's a drill we used to counteract this move; it's one I learned from my dad.

At address, we placed a ball on the

Since Norman now leaves a larger portion of his right foot on the ground, he has more control over his tee shots.

ground just to the inside of his right heel. Through impact, I asked Greg to visualize that the right heel should stay ahead of the toe of the foot, so that at impact the heel might just nudge the ball forward a bit. This monitoring device really helped Greg get the feel of the correct hip and leg action on the downswing.

The result of these setup and swing adjustments is that Greg Norman regained his position as one of the best pure ball strikers in the world. I don't believe you can pick any *one* player as the absolute best, because it's a constant tug of war. But I do think Greg will be among the best for years to come.

I think another important point for the amateur to remember is that by concentrating on the mechanics and working at them as religiously as Greg did, you can accomplish this type of dramatic improvement at any time in your golfing career. Greg started making these changes at about the time he turned 37—certainly not old, but he wasn't a kid anymore, either. So I don't care if you are 17, 32, 47, or 65; I believe that understanding the mechanics of a sound, balanced setup and swinging action will help anybody.

Next, let's talk about the work we did on Greg's pitching game and what you can learn in that area as well.

Learn to "Nip" Your Pitches

I'll bet you've always wished that you could hit your wedge shots like Greg Norman used to—that is, hit down on the ball sharply with a powerful blow that sends the ball soaring and spinning rapidly in flight, so that when it lands on the green, it "sucks back" 10 or 20 feet from where it landed, sometimes more. Greg used to do this all the time, and the fans loved it. In fact, once, in the Italian Open, Greg hit a shot on a par three that landed 35 feet past the stick, then spun back all the way into the hole for an ace.

Sounds fantastic, doesn't it? But let me tell you something—and understand that shortly I will discuss the differences the conditions can make in whether the ball can be made to back up or not—hitting down too hard and putting too much spin on the ball is not the best way to play your pitch shots.

Despite the hole-in-one I just mentioned, all the spin Greg put on the ball made it much harder to accomplish the main objective with the wedges, which is to knock the ball close to (or into) the hole. On PGA Tour courses, the greens are always fast and they usually have a substantial amount of slope, with the back of the green usually higher than the front. Greg was hitting pitching wedges or sand wedges that landed very close to the cup, but then would draw back well away from the hole and quite often entirely off the green and into trouble.

You might recall that when Norman lost the 1986 PGA championship on the 72nd hole at Inverness to Bob Tway's holed bunker shot, Greg hit a wedge that landed several feet short of the hole (cut near the front of the green), then zipped all the way back into the second cut of rough. If Greg had been able to make that pitch hit and stop dead, he'd have had a good chance to match Tway's birdie and at least force a playoff.

Believe me, it's enough of a task to hit pitch shots that land close to the hole. Loading the ball with spin the way Greg did just added more complicating factors to the task of making the ball finish close. In Greg's case, he had to factor in how much slope there was on the green, how fast the green was, and whether a slope would send the ball right or left as well

Greg Norman's new pitching swing: (*left to right*) address, backswing, downswing.

as backward. It's almost impossible to predict all of this accurately. How much better it is to simply hit a nice, soft wedge shot that you know will simply stop within a few feet of where it lands. This way, you can take dead aim at the pin and not concern yourself with all those other factors.

WHY NORMAN'S PROBLEM IS IMPORTANT TO YOU

If you're an average amateur player, or maybe even a pretty good one, you might be thinking that this problem doesn't pertain to you. I can just hear you saying, "I've never made the ball spin back like that in my

life. I'd like to do it once just to see it." Well, you might not be getting the same results that Greg Norman did, the kind that hurt his ability to score with the wedges; but you may very well be hitting the ball the same way he did, with the results hurting you in a different way. Let me explain.

First, on the PGA Tour the pros are playing wedge shots off what are probably the best conditioned fairways in the world. They are mowed every day to no more than a half inch in height, so the ball sits right up on top. Given dry weather, the Tour player has the perfect conditions to hit the ball a descending blow and catch it perfectly clean, loading it up with spin. You rarely, if ever, hit the ball off fairways this good.

Second, the Tour pros are playing to fast, sloped greens. Remember that in order for a ball to spin back, the green has to be quite fast and sloping toward you. If the green is slow, the grass's resistance will stop the ball from spinning back much. You may possibly play on pretty fast greens too, but probably not as quick and as sloped as on Tour.

Third, I remind you that Greg Norman played a 100-compression, soft-covered balata ball for maximum performance. This type of ball also carries the most backspin. Today, most manufacturers list the spin rates that a golf ball carries when hit by machine with a driver or a wedge. I don't know what type of ball you play, but the vast majority of amateurs now use a two-piece rather than a three-piece ball, and one that has a synthetic cover material rather than the softer balata. These balls simply will not carry as much backspin no matter how they are struck.

Fourth, consider the overall conditions you play in. If you play in the early morning and the fairways are always dewy and possibly a little long, a certain amount of moisture will get between your clubface and the ball at impact. This reduces the amount of spin on the ball even more.

So, if you add up all of these factors, it is really impossible for you to make the ball back up—even if you are hitting down sharply on the ball the way Greg Norman used to do.

HOW HITTING DOWN HURTS YOUR PITCHING

Now that you understand why you don't get the super spin Greg Norman did, let me explain how the steep downward blow hurts you too, but in a different way. The more you hit down on your shots, the harder it is to make the club contact the ball solidly. If you catch the ball too early on the descending blow, you will skull the shot. This means that the leading edge connects too high on the ball, so that the loft of the clubface is not applied to it. The result is a hot line drive that sails way over the green.

The more common result, however, is this: In hitting down, you make contact just a fraction behind the bottom of the ball instead of hitting the back of it. Because the downward arc of the clubhead is so steep, even if you were to make contact that's just a little bit heavy—say, a half inch behind the ball—you're going to catch a lot of grass and earth before the ball is actually struck. The result: the hated fat pitch that flies limply and lands well short of the green.

If you learn to hit the ball with a shallower approach on your pitches, you'll find that shots that felt a little fat will usually still finish on the green. Even if you catch the turf a little bit early, because you aren't digging with the club, not nearly as much earth gets between the clubface and the ball. This means the degree of error in the flight of the ball will be greatly reduced.

But back to the topic of backspin. When you deliver the clubface so that it hits the ball cleanly, the shallower arc means that there will be less backspin on the ball than with the sharp downward arc. That's because the sharp downward arc makes the ball slide up the clubface before it

On wedge shots, the idea is to make clean contact with the ball, "before" hitting the turf.

actually springs forward. However, keep in mind that even with a relatively shallow arc, a cleanly hit shot with a pitching wedge, sand wedge, or L-wedge will have lots of backspin, because these clubs carry anywhere from 48 to 60 degrees of loft on their clubfaces. Clean contact with a shallow arc with these clubs is all you need to hit a high, floating shot that stops almost dead where it lands.

Now that you understand why the relatively shallow arc is the right one for you as well as for Greg Norman, let's see how Greg made the right adjustments.

First, Greg made one "nonswing" adjustment: He started playing a ball that had a slightly lower spin rate, so that automatically his wedge shots would suck back a bit less.

More important, I worked to put more control into Greg's pitching swing than he previously had. Much like on his long shots, Greg's wedge swing was very upright, and it was relatively long and loose. Again, I asked Greg to widen his stance—not as wide as with the driver, of course, but wider than most golfers would use on a full pitching or sand wedge shot. The outsides of Greg's heels now span a distance only a little narrower than the width of his shoulders. The stance should be just a little open.

Greg positions the ball just ahead of center in his stance, with the hands slightly ahead of the ball rather than well ahead. This helps set him up for the desired fairly shallow downswing arc. For added control, Greg chokes down on the grip just about an inch.

Greg's backswing is now very controlled with his wedges, as you can see by looking at the photographs of his pitching technique. He takes the club back with quiet hands, fairly low to the ground. His weight moves smoothly onto his right leg, but see how well his right leg is able to stay braced because of his wider stance. There's no way Greg is going to slide off the ball.

Just as Greg does, keep the swing to three-quarter length on your pitch shots. The hips should turn about 25 degrees, the shoulders about 60 degrees, and the clubshaft should point at an angle that's halfway between perpendicular and parallel with the ground.

The key move to creating the more shallow arc into the ball is the same slide-then-turn-counterclockwise movement of the left hip that starts the downswing with the long clubs. The more rotational movement of Greg's hips means that the arms, too, will swing more around than vertically on the downswing.

The result of Greg's more compact wedge swing is that he hits the ball very solidly and crisply. Because the club is not moving down as sharply as before, he takes a shallower divot instead of a deep one with the wedges. When the conditions for the shot are perfect, Greg's ball will still fly high, but land quietly—take one hop and then perhaps spin back a little bit, or else just stop dead. He has become much more adept at getting the ball close to the hole, and I think this is reflected in the fabulous scoring averages Greg posted in 1993 1994, and 1995—68.90, 68.81, and 69.06, respectively, both tops on the PGA Tour.

In your case, following these setup and swing guidelines with the wedges will help you make contact much more consistently, and most

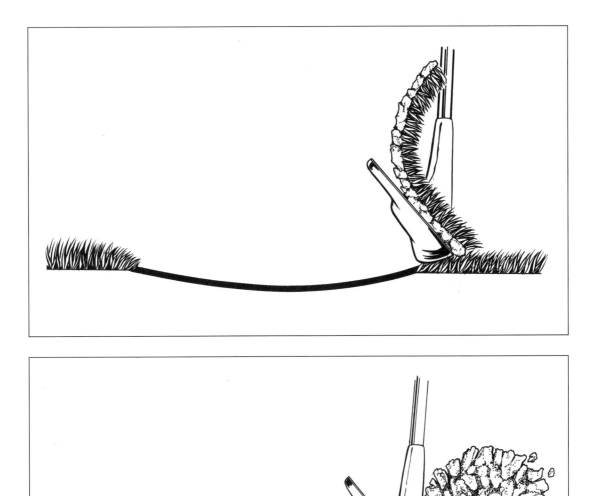

Greg now hits more controlled pitch shots because he takes a shallow divot (*top*) rather than a deep divot (*bottom*).

important, reduce or eliminate the fat shot hit with the wedge. As your confidence grows in your control with the wedges, you'll find that this will positively affect your course management approach, in that you can attack the pin more aggressively—and make more birdies.

How Norman's Putting Adjustments Can Help You

In 1992, the full swing changes that Greg and I had worked on during the previous winter had started to pay off. After Greg's relatively terrible 53rd place ranking on the 1991 money list, he climbed to number 18 in 1992. However, we agreed that while his long game was back on track, Greg's putting was still lackluster. He ranked 73rd in that category in '92, and his putting was the reason he didn't finish any higher in any of the major championships than a 6th-place showing at the Masters. Greg still had great touch, and he didn't three-putt a lot, but he wasn't making enough putts to get to the winner's circle.

So after that season I decided to sit down and take a close look at Greg's putting setup and stroke. I didn't recommend changes right away; instead, I looked at a number of tapes and photographs of many of the great putters down through the years, looking for the common elements and how Greg's method differed from theirs.

I concluded that as far as Greg's stroke was concerned, he was not moving the putterhead through the ball with a pure pendulum stroke—that is, a stroke that moves the same distance back from and past the ball. It also means one that moves the putterhead slightly inside the target line on the backstroke, onto the target line at impact, and then back slightly inside the target line on the follow-through. Instead, Greg had a tendency to swing his arms and the putter blade outward through and beyond impact, a little outside the target line, so that he was not quite getting the blade back to square at impact and was thus missing a lot of putts to the right. (Interesting, isn't it, that Greg Norman's problems on the greens were essentially of the same nature as those on his long shots—he tended to block the ball to the right?)

Be that as it may, I want to explain the changes Greg made in his grip and his posture first, because as with the full swing, the changes in the actual stroke flow from the changes in the setup.

THE "WEAK-STRONG" GRIP

Greg's stroke, like his full swing, had gotten a little bit loose, so I asked him to make a change in his grip. Instead of a standard, neutral

Norman's new putting grip.

positioning of the hands with the palms facing each other, I asked Greg to adjust to what I call a "weak-strong" hold on the club. With this grip, the left hand is turned more to the left, or underneath the club, similar to the position used by great putters like Ben Crenshaw, Corey Pavin, and Paul Azinger. When Greg's left hand was more on top of the club, his left wrist would sometimes break down through impact, which either threw the clubface off line or caused him to mishit the putt slightly.

Greg's right hand is turned to the right, into quite a strong position, which I'll grant is also a little unusual. But I asked Greg to stroke some putts with his right hand only, positioned in this manner (which is an excellent practice drill, by the way). We found that Greg moved the putterhead squarely through the ball and also hit it very solidly every time.

I believe that bringing the hands more underneath the club reduced some of the tendency of Greg's wrists to hinge during the stroke. This "weak-strong" grip promotes a stroke in which the clubhead stays low-back, low-through. This translates to a solid rap on the ball so that it rolls true and with pure overspin.

THE BENT ELBOWS SETUP

At address, you'll notice Greg's stance is moderately wide—again, a very solid position that makes it easier to stay still over the ball. Greg positions the ball just behind the inside of his left heel, which is the lowest point in the stroke. This is where you want to make contact so that impact is as solid as possible and the ball gets off to the truest possible start.

These points aside, you may notice in the photos how Greg is more flexed over the ball than he had been in the past. There is a little more bend in the knees as well as more bend from the waist. The bend from the waist helps in two ways: First, it gets Greg's eyes directly over the ball, so that he can sight directly down the target line for the truest perspective of the putt's roll. Previously, Greg's more upright position put his eyes "inside" the ball.

Norman's new putting setup is more solid.

Second, and perhaps even more important, when Greg bends from the waist, since his upper body is a little closer to the ball, it means he must bend his elbows instead of keeping them almost straight, as he had before. Bending his elbows allowed Greg to alleviate tension in his arms, and it automatically tucked his elbows in closer to his body. From this position, with his arms in close, Greg developed more of a feeling of being locked in to a pendulum stroke. Before, with his arms hanging straight down, there was no feeling of connectedness to his body. This, I'm sure, led to his tendency to swing his arms away from the body through impact and to push putts.

From Greg's new setup position, it seems that the stroke virtually takes care of itself. It is really just a miniaturized movement that's the same as his golf swing. Greg moves the club straight back from the ball, using the triangle of his hands, arms, and shoulders to move the club. There is no sensation of independent movement of anything other than the triangle, or that he is using one hand more than the other to move the club.

To return the club through the ball, Greg simply moves the triangle in the other direction through and past the ball. The putter blade stays relatively low to the ground, and because the arms and shoulders are working together, the path of the club naturally flows from slightly inside the target line on the backstroke, to square at impact, and back to slightly inside the line on the follow-through. There is no question in my mind that this is the most consistent stroking action over the long haul.

When putting, Greg now thinks of rotating the triangle formed by his arms and shoulders; on the backswing (*left*) and on the downswing (*right*). This is the mechanism that controls the movement of the putter. There is no manipulation of the club with the hands.

Greg's adjusted putting technique—plus some very dedicated hard work, I might add—has paid huge dividends. Both in 1993 and 1994, Greg vaulted back into the top ten in putting statistics, a gain that, coupled with his improved long game, has again made him arguably the world's number one player.

If you are having trouble striking your putts solidly so that they roll smoothly, and particularly if you tend to miss putts to the right, you should carefully consider the pendulum putting method that Greg is now using so well. I stated earlier that putting is a very individual part of the game of golf, so if you are rolling them in confidently and often, I wouldn't argue that you must change. But most of us aren't making the putts we think we should, so if you find yourself in this situation too, you could do a lot worse than to copy Greg Norman.

Davis Love III

LOVE'S NEW SHORT, SWEET SWING

In 1990, when Davis Love III asked me to help him fix his faulty swing, he was hitting tee shots that were flying off line and, by his standards anyway, not very far.

I found this particularly ironic, because since joining the PGA Tour in 1986, Davis was known for hitting 300-yard drives, practically on a regular basis. However, once I watched Davis swing, I quickly got a clear picture of what was going on—or rather not going on—with his technique. Instead of using his height to his advantage, as he had always done to create the widest possible swing arc, he was making some fundamental errors that were draining power from his swing.

Back then, one of Davis's major faults was swinging full out on every shot—so fast that his rhythm was out of sync. What's more, his swing was so full, and his finish so high, that he couldn't hit three-quarter shots. But Davis had more rudimentary problems, more common to a Sunday golfer than a seasoned pro. He reverse-pivoted, and he hinged his wrists too soon on the backswing. The combination of these two faults caused him to swing the club on a very narrow arc. Therefore, he was now unable to hit the ball as far as he was accustomed to hitting it. What made matters worse was that the steep backswing also caused his right wrist to collapse, or overhinge, at the top of the swing and the club to fall well below the parallel position. What he did from that point was either release the club too early on the downswing, using a "casting" action of the hands, or pull the club too sharply into the ball. Either mistake caused the ball to fly well right of the target. No wonder Davis got to the point where he started hitting irons off the tee on par-four and par-five holes.

It's important to note here that you can get away with delivering the club extra sharply into the ball when you're swinging a short iron, but not with a driver, because that club features far less loft. A driver works best when you hit with a sweeping action, rather than a descending blow.

As I mentioned in Chapter One, in Japan I gave Davis some quick tips to put his driving game back on track and raise his level of confidence. However, when we returned to the United States and started working together on home ground, I explained to him that it was time to replace the "Band-Aid" cures that I had given him earlier with some more sophisticated setup and swing keys that would take time to learn and groove. Sometimes you can become so comfortable with bad habits that they are hard to get rid of. Davis was in this very same situation, having grooved a series of fundamentally wrong positions.

In fixing Davis's problems, I remembered something my dad had taught me about teaching. He advised me to always start from the ground up when analyzing a student's problems. It's a good thing Dad told me this, because Davis's problems with swing plane and footwork had a lot to do with the way he was standing. Simply put, his stance was too narrow.

Although some golfers feel comfortable hitting short irons and touch shots from a narrower stance than others, one commonality exists among the greatest players in the world when playing tee shots: Ninety-nine percent of PGA Tour professionals spread their feet at least as wide as their shoulders. In the case of Davis Love, I noticed that the width between his feet, when measured from one inside heel to the other, was far less than the distance between his shoulders.

To understand the seriousness of this fault, stand with your feet together and swing a driver a few times. Notice how this stance causes you, or rather forces you, to swing the club virtually straight up in the air. Notice, too, that the extra narrow stance often causes you to lose your balance.

What you probably don't appreciate is how the tempo of one's

Davis Love's new wide stance has been a vital step to improving his ball striking.

swing is affected by the width of one's stance. Again, when the width of the stance is overly narrow, the tendency is to pull the club quickly upward. In turn, this quick start causes the rhythm of the backswing, as well as the downswing, to be thrown out of sync.

Professional golfers like Peter Jacobsen, Nick Faldo, Ernie Els, Greg Norman, and Ben Crenshaw realize this fact and therefore play out of a wide stance position; this gives them all a smooth takeaway action. Additionally, they are very rhythmic swingers, as were Ben Hogan, Sam Snead, Bobby Jones, and Gene Sarazen—all wide-stance players who competed during a different era.

Having diagnosed Davis's problems, albeit in light of much of the knowledge I had gained through previous conversations about the swing with my dad, I suggested some simple remedies.

My first suggestion was that the distance between Davis's feet, measured from the inside of the left heel to the inside of the right heel, be slightly greater than the distance between his shoulders. I had Davis assume such a wide stance because he is over six feet in height, and thus more susceptible to losing his balance during the swing than a shorter man. I can't support this with any formula found in a physics book; I can, however, tell you that it's true, based on my experience teaching thousands of people of different heights.

In making this change, Davis started to employ a longer takeaway action than he previously had, with the clubhead staying low to the

As these two photographs show, Davis Love now has great extension in his swing.

ground until it passed the outside of his right foot by a few inches, and until weight shifted to the inside of that foot. In fact, it is this low take-away action that encourages you to correctly shift about 75 to 80 percent of your weight to your right side during the backswing. (In contrast, when you assume a narrow stance and pick the club up quickly in the takeaway, most of your weight stays on your left foot during the back-swing. What this means, ultimately, is that most of your weight will stay on your right foot during the downswing, instead of your left foot. This fault, known as a reverse pivot, causes your shots to fly off line and not very far.)

Once Davis got a good feel for assuming a wider stance and swinging the club back low to the ground for a longer period of time, I stressed to him the importance of keeping the wrists quiet and extending his arms, hands, and club straight back. I told him that the only way to further create a wide swing arc was to maintain that extension until the clubshaft was just above level with his belt and parallel to the ground.

Once Davis reached this position, I instructed him to bring his left-arm plane down—to swing his left arm across his chest, rather than straight up in the air. This correction got rid of the tilt-and-lift action in his swing and promoted a flatter plane. My father taught me long ago that a flat swing is better than an upright swing, because it promotes a strong turning action of the body.

Next, I told Davis to swing his hands back high over his head, while feeling a comfortable firmness in his left hand and only a little bit of give in his right wrist. When he swung to the top correctly, his high-hands position maximized the width of his arc, and the club stopped at the three-quarter position. The wide arc gave him added power. The shorter swing allowed him to swing more "within himself," and thus promoted more controlled drives and iron shots. (Furthermore, it allowed him to hit more pinpoint wedge shots. Before coming to me for lessons, Davis could never have hit the wonderful wedge shots he hit close to the cup, on holes 14 and 17 at Augusta, during the final round of the 1995 Masters.)

Previously, Davis's narrow backswing forced his right wrist to collapse and the club to swing well past the parallel position. Consequently, the clubhead was so far away from the ball that he felt a sense of helplessness about returning the clubface back squarely to the ball. In response, he tended to release his hands and wrists too early and too quickly, another factor that caused him to mistime the downswing and mishit shots.

Working with Tiger Woods

Although fixing his backswing faults enabled Davis to rapidly show improvement, bettering his footwork action on the downswing enabled him to make a much smoother transition from the top of the backswing (when there is a split-second pause in the action) to the downswing. It also played a major role in getting him to hit more solid shots, as it did for Tiger Woods.

I first met Tiger Woods after he lost in the 1993 U.S. Amateur at Champions in Houston; his father wanted to bring him to me because Tiger's a big Greg Norman fan, and he knew about my work with Greg. I talked with Tiger, took some film of him, and I guess he liked what I had to say, because we've been working together ever since.

We do a lot of work over the phone; about once a month Tiger sends me tapes of his swing to analyze, and then I see him about five times a year, including visits at the majors he's playing in. The tapes are a good tool; I like to see the swing from two angles, first from behind the player looking down the line from midway between the player and the ball, and then what I call the "caddie angle," facing the player at a 90-degree angle to the line of the shot.

In our first visits, I noticed that Tiger had a problem with his right foot similar to Davis's. Tiger's, however, was more pronounced. I told Tiger that, with the swing flowing more smoothly, he'd hit the ball more solidly and accurately. Of course, Tiger being the inquisitive type, he wanted to then cut right to the chase and know what his footwork problem was.

So I gave it to him straight: "Tiger, you're too much up on your right toe during the downswing. I want more of your right foot to stay on the ground, and the heel of that foot to lead the toe. You're standing up on that right toe as if you were a ballet dancer. Until you stop it, you're going to continue to spin out on the downswing at least a couple of times in a round, hit those awful off-the-world drives that cost you double bogeys—and tournaments."

I further explained to Tiger that players whose swings stood the test of time had great footwork. I cited Sam Snead, Ben Hogan, Lee Trevino, Tom Watson, and Jack Nicklaus as the chief models for mastering good footwork. After listening to me, Tiger said he was willing to change. However, in sticking to my dad's "ground-up" teaching philosophy, I first focused on his stance rather than his footwork.

Like Davis, Tiger is tall: 6 feet 2 inches. So he had similar problems—namely, an overly long, overly steep backswing. However, I had Tiger assume an even wider stance than Davis's. I knew that this change, plus having Tiger employ a smaller hip turn, would help him shorten his swing while creating a wide arc. But, more important, a wide stance would calm his very "sloppy" right foot, and thereby improve the sequence of his entire downswing.

Because Tiger kept his left foot planted on the backswing, I wanted him to start his downswing with a bump of the left hip. When he assumed a narrow stance and allowed all but the toe end of the right foot to lift up early in the downswing, Tiger was unable to employ the proper weight-shifting and hip-shifting actions. Instead of shifting his hips laterally, then clearing them in a counterclockwise direction, Tiger's hips would spin out. This is one of the worst moves in golf. "If you spin, you'll never win," my dad used to say.

Tiger's new stance helped him keep the right foot down longer on the downswing and make a better move through the ball. However, as I told Tiger, there's still room for improvement.

Swinging too fast is one of the other causes of an overactive right foot and straightening the right leg before impact. To tame Tiger, I told him to concentrate on swinging at 75 percent of his full-out speed. Additionally, I had him hit a lot of flat-footed punch shots.

In addition to allowing Tiger to hit pro-quality tee shots, his new swing enables him to play more controlled long and medium iron shots. Because his action is far less steep, he doesn't dig down into the turf anymore. When you do dig down, grass and dirt get lodged between the grooves of the clubface at impact, causing the ball to fly as much as 20 yards farther than normal.

Tiger's new swing, employing both the big and small muscles of the body, enables him to hit long and medium irons with more of a sweeping action than digging action. Therefore, it's a fluke if he hits a flyer from fairway grass. Moreover, because his distance control is not affected by the flyer, he can judge his iron shots more precisely. (Having said that, one important thing Tiger has to learn is how to hit three-quarter short-iron shots "under the gun." At Augusta, he got overly pumped up, which caused him to hit a couple of short irons over the green. Had he been better able to control both the length of his swing and his emotions, he'd have hit even more good shots, and finished even higher up the leaderboard. Still, not bad for a man not yet 21 years of age.)

Tiger's New Swing

Although Tiger's swing is not perfect just yet, it's rated among the very best by experts. For this reason, I'd like you to take a close look at some of the key positions of Tiger's swing, so that I can point out those things that are as important to hitting the ball solidly today as they were when my dad was standing on the practice tee, giving lessons at Winged Foot, Seminole, or Thunderbird.

Address:

Note Tiger's wide stance. This solid foundation lets him make a powerful on-balance swing.

Note, also, Tiger's strong grip. This hold sets the forearms in the ideal position at address. In turn, this setup enables him to swing the club back on a shallow path and, ultimately, release it more freely and proficiently.

The Extension:

Note the firmness of Tiger's wrists. By delaying the cocking action of the wrists, he's able to extend the club farther back. The farther the

Tiger Woods in the address position. (See the text for a detailed analysis of Tiger's swing.)

In the extension position.

extension action, the wider the swing arc; the wider the swing arc, the more power you generate.

At this point in the swing, the upper part of the left arm brushes against the side of the chest. Also, the right leg maintains its posture, with some "healthy" tension being felt in the right foot and leg.

At the Top:

Note Tiger's three-quarter swing position. I'm happy to say that my three star students, Greg Norman, Davis Love, and Tiger Woods—all

Tiger Woods at the top of the swing.

Starting down.

now employ this length action, one big reason why statistics now show that they hit the ball with excellent control. They'll never be accused of being driving wimps, either.

In Tiger's case, a smaller hip turn helped him shorten his swing.

Start Down:

At this point in the swing, Tiger leaves a lot more of his right foot on the ground. Before he came to me for lessons, he was totally up on his toes during the start of the downswing. This new position enables him to

In the impact position.   In the follow-through position.

make a solid shift of the hips. Before, when he was "dancing," the hips spun out, causing a loss of balance. To be honest, however, even now there's still some room for improvement. I'd like to see Tiger be even more "grounded" than he already is.

Impact:

Tiger's head has rotated back to a straight up-and-down position. The head weighs about 25 pounds, so it's important that you let it have a swing of its own. Tiger's head rotation on the downswing allows him to transfer his weight onto his left foot and put all his weight and power behind the shot.

F o l l o w - T h r o u g h :

After impact, Tiger's right arm rotates over his left arm. (Many amateurs are under the misconception that *before* impact the right hand releases over the left hand. This is one of the chief reasons they mishit the ball.)

Note, also, the firmness of Tiger's left leg. It proves he hits against a firm left side, as do all power hitters.

Serious Faults and

CHAPTER FIVE

Simple Fixes

YOU CAN CURE GOLF'S

MOST COMMON SHOTMAKING FAULTS—

THE TOO-FAST SWING, THE TOP,

THE SKY, THE DUCK HOOK,

THE SLICE, AND THE SHANK

If you feel you have mastered all the elements of the long game, as described in Chapter Two, then you may not have to read this chapter. You will have developed a secure grip, a sound, well-balanced setup, and from these, a golf swing that is as powerful as your physique allows. Just as important, your swing will be repetitive. You should be able to strike the ball with a reasonable degree of consistency, if not quite like Greg Norman or Davis Love III.

Unfortunately, I realize that many of you may still be subject to—and in some cases literally afraid of—the "disaster shots" of golf, which include the topped shot, the slice, and (dare I say it?) the shank. So, in this chapter, my goal is to discuss the specific full-shot faults that plague so many golfers, and to help you fix at least one shot that may be killing your enjoyment of the game.

Why Do We Swing So Fast?

I have given thousands of lessons to amateur golfers, and I would estimate that at least 50 percent of them swing the club faster than they should.

To execute a good golf swing, you have to give the large muscles in your body time to do their work. We have talked about the most effective golf swing being one in which the action is controlled by the large muscles, rather than the small muscles of the hands and wrists. Well, in order to make a golf swing that utilizes the big muscles of the legs, hips, and torso, the entire action from start to finish should take at least 1.6 seconds. I would say that if it takes around two full seconds, so much the better.

I'll bet the majority of golfers' full swings take less than a second and a half. There's no way in that little time for them to get their weight shifted well to the right side, then make a good combination lateral/rotational move with the hips to start the downswing.

Why do most amateurs swing so fast? I think it stems from two things. First, many amateurs have not had the proper instruction on the mechanics of the swing. They don't know how to use the big muscles to swing the club, so they make a quick flail at it with their hands. If you've absorbed everything in this book to this point, you can't say that this lack of knowledge is the cause of the problem.

The second thing that produces overly fast swings is anxiety. Most amateurs are very anxious about the result of their upcoming swing and rush it, either to see how the ball will fly, or maybe just to get the shot over with.

If you've just realized that you are one of those 50 percent of all golfers who swing too fast for their own good, I'd like to show you some mental and physical cues that will help you slow down your golf swing and give it a chance to function at top level.

1. Make a Slow Practice Swing.

Before stepping up to any full shot, make a very slow practice swing, at no more than 75 percent of the speed you think you normally swing. Then, step up to the ball and try to hit the shot at that same pace, at 75 percent of your normal tempo. Just trust yourself and do it, à la Davis Love III.

I think you'll be very surprised at the results of this tactic. You'll probably think, heck, I'll only hit the ball 75 percent as far as normal. But trust it; I'll bet you hit your most solid shot of the day, for your maximum distance.

The trick to this drill, I've found, is that even when you promise yourself to swing at 75 percent of full throttle, you'll actually swing at between 80 and 90 percent of your normal tempo, and this is generally just right for you if swinging too fast has been your problem. So discipline yourself to make a three-quarter-speed practice swing, then repeat it on the actual shot.

2. Make Your Backswing and Downswing Speeds "Match."

A lot of golfers who swing too fast may not be too quick taking the club back, but are blindingly fast coming down. In other words, their backswing and downswing speeds don't "match." You can't make a downswing that fully utilizes your lower body if the downswing is only slightly slower than the speed of light!

Make a conscious effort to make your backswing and downswing speeds identical. Count to yourself as you make the swing: "One-and-two," with "one" being for the backswing, "and" representing the top of the swing, and "two" representing your downswing. Try to swing your arms down and through the ball at exactly the same speed with which you brought them back. Don't worry about how far you'll hit the ball. Even though you're swinging your arms back down in what feels like a leisurely fashion, the centrifugal force built up in the shaft and clubhead will be releasing in the impact zone. You'll be surprised how solidly and how far you hit it when you even out the tempo between your backswing and your downswing.

3. Hum a Tune.

This is more of a mental tip, but one that many golfers find helpful. Simply hum a tune as you make your practice swing, step up to the ball, and play the shot. This should set you into a relaxed frame of mind to start with as you prepare the shot. It should give you a better chance to stay relaxed and to produce a smooth tempo during the actual swing.

Make sure that as you execute the shot, you keep humming your tune at its normal pace and with a normal amount of effort in your voice. At first you might notice as you start the swing that the sound of your voice tightens or intensifies. This indicates tension that usually transfers into tightness and/or quickness during the swing, so it's a good indicator that you need to stay mentally and physically relaxed throughout the swinging process.

4. Hit Shots With Your Feet Together.

On the practice tee, if you sense that you've been swinging too fast or too hard, a great drill is to hit shots with your feet together. Use no longer than a middle iron for this exercise—a 5-, 6-, or 7-iron would be fine. If it helps your confidence, feel free to tee the ball up. Then set up to the ball normally, except that your heels are touching or nearly touching. Go ahead and swing.

You'll quickly discover two things doing this drill: (1) that you must swing with good balance (or else you'll fall over); (2) that in order to swing in good balance, you must swing slowly and smoothly. I recommend that you make it a habit to hit some balls with your feet together on the practice tee, if not every time you practice, then perhaps every second or third time. Don't concern yourself at all with how far the shots go (although I think you'll be surprised that they still get out there a good way when you just hit the shot squarely).

5. Swing at Imaginary Practice Balls.

Again on the practice tee, take a middle iron and tee up a ball. Then step a few feet to the left of the teed-up ball, and make a leisurely practice swing at an imaginary ball. Repeat this swing at an imaginary ball five times, each time stepping forward a few inches toward the actual ball, as if each of the imaginary balls had been set up in a line. Finally, set your clubhead down behind the real ball and simply make your sixth smooth, leisurely swing in this sequence. Just let the ball get in the way of that nice smooth swing. I think you'll agree that the feeling of the swing at the real ball is a lot slower and smoother than the swings you've been making out on the course.

6. "Chip" the Driver.

This one might sound a little odd, but it will help you if you're swinging too fast. Tee up the ball on the practice tee and, with your driver, make a nice, leisurely "chip" swing. Just try to tap it out there about 75 yards. Hit a half-dozen chip shots like this with your driver.

Next, hit some slightly longer "chips," about 100 yards, using the same slow, leisurely quarter-to-half swing. After several more of these, extend the swing slightly farther, to pitching distance, still using the driver, and hit some nice easy shots that travel a total of 150 yards. Hit about eight or ten balls this way.

Finally, let's assume that your normal, respectable drive travels something over 200 yards. It doesn't matter if it's 220 yards, 240 yards, whatever. Continuing to make a smooth, leisurely pass at the ball, just try to hit some soft drives out there about 180 yards. Nothing more. Hit as many balls as you like doing this.

I think you'll be surprised that two things happen. First, when you try to smooth it out there about 180, you'll strike the ball very solidly—and hit it a lot farther than 180 yards. You'll probably hit the ball just about as far as your best with your normal swing—and a lot more consistently. Second, this entire exercise will ingrain a slower, more even tempo into your swing—because you have eliminated what brings the speed into the swing in the first place: the perceived need to hit the ball hard.

7. Swing With Your Eyes Closed.

This is an exercise that Dad used, both with his students and to keep his own swing at a smooth pace. Tee up the ball, again using the driver and, after going through your normal preshot routine, simply close your eyes and swing. Give yourself a few tries to get over the anxiety that this sightless swing usually causes. I think you'll find that your instincts for where the ball is will kick into play and you'll start meeting the ball surprisingly well.

More important though, I guarantee that when you swing at the ball with your eyes closed, you'll swing the club slowly and smoothly. It's as though, without the benefit of sight, your subconscious realizes that you have to rely on clubhead control and good tempo to meet the ball well, and that's what you'll create as you swing the club.

It's quite likely that by slowing down your swing using the seven exercises described, you'll go a long way toward eliminating the faulty shots I'm about to describe. However, you may feel you need a little more specific assistance in ridding yourself of these hated misses, so let's discuss them individually.

Topped Shot With a Wood

Topping the ball is probably the most humiliating way to miss a golf shot. It might not actually be the worst way to miss the ball, because usually when somebody tops it, the ball rolls out there fairly straight (hopefully there isn't a water hazard in front of you). So the player is not out of bounds or in the woods; he or she has just lost a lot of distance. Still, topped shots seem as though they're the worst way to miss a shot simply because the player did not get the ball up into the air.

I believe that the primary cause of topped shots lies more in the setup and only partly in the swing itself. This setup flaw is that with the woods, most golfers stand too far away from the ball. This occurs, I believe, because most golfers have the mistaken impression that if they stand farther from the ball, they'll be in a more powerful position (not true). Or sometimes they have the mistaken impression that because the club is longer, they have to bend over more and outstretch their arms. Although it's true that you should stand a bit farther from the ball with the longer clubs, it is not true that you should alter your posture dramatically.

At any rate, when you start the swing from a "reaching" position, your intuition will tell you that you're starting to lean too much toward the ball and that you will lose your balance. So what usually happens is the player instinctively stands up a little as the backswing progresses and then transitions into the downswing. This instinctive "standing up" movement, in an effort to retain balance, is enough to cause you to top the ball. Remember, the golf ball is only 1.687 inches in diameter. If the leading edge of the club catches the ball at its equator or higher, the shot will be a top. You need only raise your spine up about three quarters of an inch to an inch from its starting point at address, and assuming you make no other adjustments, the result will be a topped shot.

The Cure.

Simply stand a little closer to the ball with your wood clubs. I can't tell you how much closer because every individual is different, but you may only need to adjust by an inch or two. Make sure that with the clubhead squarely behind the ball, your arms are hanging naturally and without any tension. As you swing the club back, key on maintaining the flex in your right knee and also on "swinging around your spine." There should be no sense of lifting in any part of your body on the backswing.

As you head into the downswing, your only thought (after shifting your weight onto your forward foot) should be to swing your arms through the ball freely. Never try to consciously use your hands to hit at the ball. This can cause sufficient tension that might keep your wrists from fully uncocking, which is another reason, albeit a less likely one, for the clubhead to come into the ball slightly above ground level.

To understand your topping problem with irons, look at the difference between the "reverse pivot" (*left*) and a solid weight-shift action (*right*).

Again, try swinging with your eyes closed. This drill will help prevent you from becoming "ball-bound," hitting "at" the ball, and topping shots. You'll learn to make a fluid swing "through" the ball, with your head and eyes rotating out of the shot through impact.

Topped Shot With an Iron

Again, standing too far from the ball with an iron can cause the topped shot, but I think more shots are topped or badly "thinned" with the irons because of the biggest swing fault in golf: the *reverse pivot*. For the right-handed golfer, this means that he or she keeps too much weight on the left foot at the top of the backswing, and then reverses too much weight onto the right foot, away from the target, on the downswing. In addition to a loss of power, this causes the lowest point in the swing to occur behind the ball. If the player doesn't catch the ground first and hit the shot fat, he or she will catch the ball on the upswing, blading or topping the shot.

I think this fault is common with the irons because the average golfer, who watches the pros hit high, soft iron shots to the flag, instinctively believes that the ball has to be lifted into the air with a flick of the wrists to achieve such height on these approach shots. The high-handicapper doesn't really trust correct swing mechanics plus the loft on the clubface to do the job.

T h e   C u r e .

At the practice range, tee up the ball about one-half inch. With a middle iron, concentrate on getting your weight onto your right side on the backswing; then, try to cut the tee in half underneath the ball rather than focusing on the ball itself. Don't worry about how well you hit the shot; just cut the tee in half underneath the ball.

By shifting your weight to the right on the backswing and then trying to cut down the tee, you have to deliver a descending blow rather than an ascending one. This drill almost forces you to get your weight onto your left side as you should, rather than hanging back on your right side and trying to scoop the shot.

Whenever you find yourself slipping back into a reverse weight shift and the not-so-solid shots that go with it, return to this drill in your next

To cure a topping problem, hit shots off a tee with a 5-iron.

practice session; or concentrate on turning your left shoulder over your right knee.

Skying the Ball Off the Tee

In order for the tee shot to carry a good distance, the ball's initial trajectory must be fairly low. In reality, a well-hit shot will shoot out at an angle slightly lower than the loft on the club you're using. In the case of a driver, this means the starting trajectory should be 9 or 10 degrees; with a 3-wood, perhaps a 13- or 14-degree launch angle.

Most amateurs get unsatisfactory distance off the tee because they pop up or "sky" most of their tee shots. Instead of shooting the ball out on a low, rising trajectory, they hit bloopers that fly like a 9-iron or a wedge.

The cause of the skied tee shot is that the player is not delivering the metal driver's loft squarely into the back of the ball. Instead, the player chops down on the ball, the opposite of the scooping action just discussed for the topped iron. The top of the clubface hits the ball, but it does so while it's traveling sharply downward. This glancing blow transfers less forward momentum to the ball, and also puts unwanted backspin on it, making the ball soar high and short. Result: a tee shot that travels only 50 to 60 percent as far as your solid hit would have.

The Cure.

You need to make a shallower delivery of the clubhead through the hitting zone. Here's an image to help you: Tee up the ball normally. Then imagine there's a second ball teed up about two inches in front of the real one. Concentrate on swinging right through the real ball and hitting the imaginary ball solidly.

You couldn't possibly make a level swing through impact with that imaginary ball if you were still hitting down sharply on the real one. This drill helps rid you of the main physical flaw that causes the steep downswing to begin with: overuse of the hands, arms, and shoulders in an attempt to "muscle" the ball.

Try to hit the imaginary ball solidly, and you'll sweep through the actual ball as well, and start getting the best possible trajectory on your tee shots.

Weak Pop-Ups With the Irons

The player who hits high, weak shots with the irons, without actually hitting the ground behind the ball, is able to catch the ball neatly just at the bottom of the swing. However, he or she is still staying back on the right side too much through the impact zone, and is usually releasing the right hand underneath the left at impact, so that the clubhead scoops the ball up higher into the air than the true loft of the clubface. The ball's initial trajectory is much too high, with the ball flying limply into the air rather than describing a piercing flight in which the ball starts low and rises to a peak later. This kind of impact hurts your shotmaking most with the longer irons, and makes it very hard to control the ball in windy conditions.

The Cure.

This player must make a more conscious effort to make a solid weight shift from the right side to the left on the downswing. You should never have the feeling of hanging back on your iron shots. Remember to bump the left hip toward the target to initiate the downswing. Also, work on your extension of the clubhead through the ball. In order to keep the clubhead low, think of straightening your right arm through the ball as opposed to curling your right hand underneath your left. The more you can extend your right arm, the more level the clubhead will stay; and coupled with an improved weight transfer, you'll get a slightly downward clubhead path leading into the impact zone, which will let you contact the ball first and apply backspin and control to the shot.

Fat Shots With the Fairway Woods

There can be several causes for hitting the ball "fat" with the fairway woods, but one of the more common ones I see is the result of a lack of control of the clubhead at the top of the backswing.

Many amateurs swing up to the top, then, in straining to make the club get back a little farther (in trying to get extra distance, no doubt) they let go of the club with the last three fingers of the left hand. The club wobbles behind them for an instant; then the player snatches the club tightly at the start of the downswing. This snatching move triggers a steep downswing that is all hands and arms, in which the most likely result is pulling the club down into the turf behind the ball.

If you wear a glove, there's a good way to find out whether you are loosening your hold on the club at the top, then "grabbing" on the way down: Check the pad of your golf glove (the lower-right quadrant of a glove on the left hand). Is there a rough spot of wear there? If so, this almost surely means you are gripping and regripping at the top.

The Cure.

At address, grip the club relatively firmly, with equal pressure in both hands. Make some swings while trying to maintain the same pressure throughout the swing as you started with at address. Feel the same amount of control of the golf club throughout the entire swinging motion. This will help you eliminate the "grab" at the top and the chopping downswing motion that follows it. In turn, this will make your downswing path with the fairway woods more sweeping, as it needs to be.

A final point: Remember my advice in Chapter Two, in which I suggested that you make a backswing turn that is just three quarters of your maximum swing. Don't try to extend your backswing to the absolute "max." Regripping the club as described here is one of the negative side-effects of trying to get the club farther back than your body really allows you to. If you want to extend your backswing, do it the right way, by working on your flexibility—not artificially by letting go of the club.

Fat Shots With Irons

Again, there can be a number of causes of fat iron shots. One of the main ones is a backswing in which there is no width, no extension of the clubhead behind the player, and correspondingly a very steep downswing in which the clubhead is almost certain to take too much turf.

In addition to not getting the weight onto the right side correctly on the backswing, which contributes to a narrow rather than a wide arc,

The "broken" left arm position is the chief cause of fat iron shots.

To prevent fat shots with irons, keep your left arm relatively straight during the backswing.

many players bend the left or lead arm excessively, again in an effort to get the club well back behind them. Usually when someone bends the left arm drastically, he or she will cast the club back down very steeply. It's almost impossible to hit a clean shot with an arc that's too steep.

The Cure.

Try to push the club straight back from the ball for the first 12 inches, while keeping the triangle of your arms and shoulders intact. Then allow the club to gradually extend inside the target line as the backswing progresses, keeping your left arm in control of the movement. I don't want to advise you to keep the left arm really tight, as this can upset the smoothness of the swing. But you should feel as though your left arm is controlling the clubshaft as it moves through the backswing. A tiny bit of give near the top of the backswing is okay. But meanwhile you will have built a nice wide backswing arc and be in a good position to deliver the club on a shallower but still-descending plane into the ball. In turn, you'll be in much better position to nip the ball off the turf with just a small divot, rather than digging deep.

Duck Hook With the Woods

The "duck hook," with the possible exception of the shank, is the ugliest shot in golf. This is the shot that starts low and well left of the target, and then quickly turns even farther left before diving into the ground.

The flight of the duck-hooked shot clearly describes the swing flaws that have occurred. The path of the clubhead through impact came from outside the target line to inside—otherwise the ball would not have started to the left—and the clubface was delofted and closed at impact, even in relation to that outside-in swing path, as is shown by the fact that the ball dove even farther left.

So what are the flaws in the duck-hook swing? First, the player is likely not getting enough shoulder rotation into his or her backswing. Instead of making a good shoulder turn that gets the club behind him or her, the player shoves the club back, outside the target line. Coming down, the golfer compounds the error by casting the club toward the ball with the hands, shutting the clubface so that the ball ends up going "left to left."

Coming down with a "lazy" lower body and a shut clubface can cause you to hit a left-to-left shot with a wood.

To cure the duck hook, make sure to let the lower body lead the downswing.

The Cure.

Make sure to keep the backswing slow, and rotate your shoulders in clockwise fashion. Although I told you in Chapter Two that most players would benefit by swinging within themselves on the backswing, for the person fighting the duck hook I would advise an increase in the shoulder turn. Try to turn your shoulders 90 degrees from your starting position, so that the clubhead gradually moves inside the target line and then behind you on the backswing.

Once you've made a good turn and gotten the club behind you, again key on starting the downswing from the ground up—lower body first! If you make that lateral hip "bump," and get your weight on your left side as your first move, there is no way you will cast the club and close the clubface. The clubhead will stay inside the target line on the downswing and be pulled into the ball squarely at impact.

Duck Hook With the "Longer" Irons

Some golfers may also hit duck hooks with the longer irons, say, the 2-, 3-, 4-, and 5-irons. (Fortunately, it's almost impossible to hit a duck hook with the 6-iron or higher. The reason is that when a club has a higher loft than a 5-iron, it's hard to flip the club closed enough so that the ball will fly left to left, then dive into the ground the way a duck hook does. If you were to make the duck-hook swing moves, with say, a 7- or 8-iron, what you'd probably get is a straight pull to the left and a ball trajectory that looked more like that of a 4- or 5-iron.)

It's definitely possible to duck-hook the longer irons, though. This fault is caused by independent hand action on the backswing and/or downswing that delivers the club in such a shut position through impact that the ball starts left and never really gets up in the air.

The Cure.

The late Jimmy Demaret, when asked by an amateur what to do to cure his slice, used to simply quip, "Hook it." Similarly, my answer to the problem of solving the duck hook is simply to start slicing it! Ben Hogan used to practice deliberate slices all the time to retrain his muscles any time he was pulling or hooking the ball.

To reprogram yourself to hit the deliberate slice, make the following adjustments: First, align your body slightly left of the target at address. Next, increase the grip pressure in your left hand. This will assist you in controlling the shot with your left hand and arm, rather than letting your right hand take over at the start of the downswing and flip the clubface closed.

Push the club away on the backswing slightly outside the target line, with your left arm and shoulder controlling the action, so that you swing the club into a more upright top-of-swing position. On the downswing, pull down firmly along the alignment of your body, which is slightly outside-in in relation to your target line, with your left arm in control. If you've been duck-hooking, you may have to exaggerate this outside-in slicing feeling for a while. Keep at it, and eventually you'll get the ball starting left of your target line, then curving right, toward the target. Once you get to the point that you are getting this result, I don't think you'll be able to duck-hook the ball even if you tried.

Slicing With Woods and Long Irons

It's difficult to hit a big, left-to-right slice with the short irons. That's because the higher the degree of loft on the clubface, the more backspin is imparted to the ball. And the more backspin a shot carries, the less that sidespin, in this case left-to-right sidespin, can act on the ball's flight and make it curve right. (Incidentally, this is why so many students tell me, "I'm hitting my short irons really well; now if I can only figure out my slice with the long clubs!" They are actually making pretty much the same slice swing with all their clubs; it just doesn't show as much with the short irons.)

Usually, the really struggling slicer has what I call an "action-reaction" swing. You've heard the statement in school or perhaps read it in science books, "For every action there's an equal and opposite reaction." Well, in this case, the initial action is that of swinging the club way inside the target line on the backswing. Instead of moving that upper body triangle straight back from the ball to start the backswing, the player whips the club way inside the target line with his or her hands.

As a reaction to this inside move on the backswing, the player then makes a big looping over-the-top move to start the downswing, throwing the clubhead way outside the target line. This brings the clubhead into the ball from an outside-in angle and also from a steep angle. The result is a glancing blow, left-to-right sidespin, and a weak, sliced shot.

An overly flat takeaway can cause you to slice wood shots.

The Cures.

There are really four cures for the basic slice. You may find that one of them can solve your slice better than another, or that working on all four solutions will help.

The first cure is simply to move the club, on the backswing, straight back away from the ball, rather than flipping it quickly to the inside. Then simply make the best shoulder turn you can to work the club gradually inside the target line. If you take the club back nice and square, you may very well eliminate that reactive downswing move in which you throw the clubhead to the outside. Simply try to start down with your lower body first, then make your downswing path retrace your backswing path as closely as you can.

The second slice cure is to make sure that you utilize your hands and forearms correctly during the downswing. Remember that even in a good downswing, as the clubhead approaches the ball, the clubface will

Employing a straight takeaway is one sure way to prevent hitting slice shots.

be looking open in relation to the target line. Some golfers, especially those who tend to hold the club in a death grip, don't have enough freedom in their arm swing to square up the clubface.

While I don't want you to think in terms of flipping the clubface closed with your hands, an improved rotation of the forearms through impact may work wonders. After starting down with the left hip leading the way, simply rotate your right forearm smoothly over your left forearm. This will move the clubface into a square position at impact and a closed position (in relation to the target line) slightly beyond impact.

If you find that you need a little additional help to get the clubface squared up at impact, you can aid your release by practicing with a "split grip" in place of your standard grip. Simply place your right hand on the club underneath your left with at least two inches of space between the bottom of your left hand and the top of your right. Since this will feel a bit odd, aid your confidence during this drill by teeing the ball up and using a 5-iron. Again, try to cross your right forearm over your left through the impact zone.

Keeping the right hand well below your left on the handle will make the right hand feel much more in charge of the action and will aid you in making the forearm crossover move. Hit about 10 to 20 balls in this fashion. Then go back to your normal grip, again making sure to cross the right forearm over the left through impact. Your shots should fly straighter. In fact, I wouldn't be surprised if some follow a controlled-draw flight pattern.

The third slice cure for you to try is as follows: Tee the ball up for a shot with your driver or 3-wood. Set up to the ball in your normal address position. Once you have done this, turn your body into an extremely closed position. Your hips and shoulders should be about 45 degrees closed so that your back is substantially facing the target. Your arms should still be holding the clubhead behind the ball, but the rest of you should be turned into a severely closed position.

As you can imagine, it will be difficult to get the club back to the ball, while still swinging along the target line, from this body position. You'll want to swing the club more along the line your body is pointing

Hitting driver (*above*) or 3-wood shots from an extremely closed address position is one of the most inventive ways to cure the slice with woods.

than along the target line, which feels like it's way left. However, keep striving to unwind your torso fully on the downswing, so that you are getting the clubhead onto the ball moving more or less along the target line. Don't worry about how far the ball goes or what the shot looks like.

Just keep your body turning actively through the downswing so that you are delivering the clubhead to the ball.

Try to hit 20 balls or so from this position. Then tee up some balls and hit shots with your driver or 3-wood from your normal address position. Notice how the fact that you were forced to keep turning and turning through the downswing from that ultra-closed position now makes it seem much easier to turn through the shot when you're lined up at the target—and, at the same time, to square up the clubface so you hit a straight shot or a draw.

The fourth slice cure is to practice "opposites." In other words, purposely practice hitting hooks. You'll be surprised how fast this drill will iron out your faulty swing path and plane. (Severe "hookers" should practice hitting slices.)

The Shank

Finally, we come to the type of missed shot that many high-handicappers—and even some better golfers, too—have come to dread most. The shank is the shot that golfers talk about in hushed tones, or sometimes won't even talk about at all, for fear that even talking about the shank will make them start actually shanking the ball.

A shanked shot is one in which contact is made between the ball and the hosel of an iron club, as opposed to the clubface itself. The shank can only be hit with an iron, not a metalwood, because the basic design of the metalwood does not place the hosel in front of the clubface as with an iron.

The shanked ball, when contacted on the inside of the rounded hosel area, squirts away wildly to the right of the target—as much as 50 to 60 degrees off line to the right. The worst-looking shanks will occur with the shortest irons or the wedges. This is because the greater the loft on the club, the more the inside of the hosel is exposed.

An out-to-in swing path is the major cause of this shank shot.

Most golfers believe that the shank occurs because the player allows his or her hands to get way ahead of the shot on the downswing, so the hosel leads the clubface into the ball. While this is a possibility, in my experience most shanks occur primarily because of an out-to-in swing path. The player casts the club to the outside starting down, rather than initiating the downswing move with the lower body. Often, this outside move with the arms and upper body is enough to throw the player's balance a little toward the toes, so that the clubhead is delivered a little outside the ball with its face closed. If it's an iron club you're swinging, a shank can be the result.

You might find it interesting to note (and I'm not trying to scare you here) that it does not take a dramatic error to shank a ball with an iron. This was probably more true with the classic forged irons that predominated ten or more years ago, as opposed to the perimeter-weighted, oversized irons that have become popular today. The reason is, with a forged blade and no perimeter weighting, the sweet spot of the clubhead was actually on the hosel side of the center of the clubface—not the dead center of the clubface itself. And since the face itself was somewhat smaller than in most irons we see today, this meant the perfect hit with the forged blade was actually pretty close to the hosel. So a good golfer might make what felt like not too bad a swing, maybe getting just a little outside on the downswing, yet out of the blue get a shocker of a shank as a result. As I said, one of the benefits of modern iron club design is that the clubheads are larger from heel to toe. With more weight out toward the toe, the

To cure the shank, practice hitting with a head cover outside the ball.

sweet spot is much closer to, if not exactly on, the geometric center of the clubface. I think that one of the benefits of modern iron design is that you're a little less likely to shank the ball if you throw the club outside the ball through the impact zone.

Still, people certainly suffer from shanked shots, so let me propose a couple of cures that have worked well with my students.

Cure #1.

On the practice tee, place a clubhead cover (or a small cardboard box) just two inches to the outside of the ball. Use any club from a 9-iron to a 5-iron. If you've been shanking the ball, you'll hit the object next to the ball with the toe of the club. Keep hitting iron shots, focusing on keeping your swing path moving from inside the target line (prior to entering the hitting area) along the target line at impact. The mental cue of having the small object outside the ball will encourage you to swing the club along this plane. Keep hitting balls in this manner for several sessions, even after you have cured the shank, as it is a good general reminder to ensure solid contact.

Cure #2.

If you're really struggling with shanked shots, consider addressing the ball more toward the toe of the club.

On the surface, this cure might seem like a "Band-Aid" in that you may think its sole purpose is to address the ball with the shank farther away from it. Of course, you don't want to hit the ball way out on the toe either. That type of contact will give you poor results also, although not as poor as a shank. No, the real reason for addressing the ball more toward the toe is that doing so will encourage an inside-out swing path, just as the object-beside-ball drill does.

Address the ball toward the toe with a middle or short iron. Make your normal backswing, being sure to shift your weight onto your right side. Next, as you swing into impact, extend the club from the inside back to the ball, then through it. If you learn to deliver the club from inside the target line prior to impact, not only will your shanking problems be over, but all your iron shots will feel much more solid.

Afterword

Throughout this book we have covered various methods you can use to help improve your overall game. Good, consistent play begins with mastering the four cornerstones; concentrate on each of these areas, and soon you'll be shooting lower scores. Your lesson doesn't end here, however. You must take this knowledge to the golf course and practice what we've covered here. If you use this book as a way to understand your basic golf flaws, and as a tool for correcting them, you'll certainly further your love for the game.

In the end, I hope this book helps you as much as I've been helped throughout my career by some very special people. I have been exceptionally fortunate my whole life to have been able to learn from the very best professionals in the game. Without their willingness to share their knowledge of the golf swing, I would not be in a position to share my own thoughts with you. I offer them my sincere gratitude for their infinite wisdom and help. They are:

Claude Harmon
Tommy Armour
Craig Wood
Ben Hogan
Jackie Burke
Dave Marr
John Jacobs
Lambert Topping
Jim McLean
Craig Harmon
Dick Harmon
Bill Harmon
David Leadbetter
Mike McGetric

Index

iron clubs:
  duck hook and, 235–36
  fat shot and, 232–33, *232*
  shank and, 241–44, *242, 243*
  topped shot with, *226,* 227, *228*
  weak pop-up with, 230
iron shots, 24
  hitting of, 172–73
  tip for, 164

J

Jacobsen, Peter, 207
Jones, Robert Trent, 32, 207

K

Kite, Tom, 58, 94
knees to chest, 133

L

Laffoon, Ky, 151
lag putt, 177
left arm position, fat shots with irons
    and, 232–33, *232*
left-heel lift, 77, 79, 163
  backswing and, 174
"left-in-the-bunker" shots, 113
lies, 89, 96, 120, 126
  grassy, 171
  sand and grass, 170
  uphill vs. downhill, 163
lob wedge (L-wedge), 92, 197
  tip on use of, 168
Lochinvar Golf Club, 126, 146
loft, of club, 88, 92, 117, 127, 197
long game:
  elements of, 43–83
  faults and fixes to, 217–44
  goals of, 219
long putts, mishitting of, 176
Love, Davis, Jr., 35
Love, Davis, III, 12, 35–37, *39,* 71, 119
  club selection and, 124–25
  swing of, 205–10, *207, 208*
low iron shot, 172
low punch shot, 61

low shot, overhanging branches and,
    171

M

Marr, Dave, 13, 22, 34
Masters, 11, 17–19, *18,* 21, 37, 57, 145,
    167–68
Mayer, Dick, 22
Mayfield, Shelly, 13
Meadow Brook Club, 24
mental game, 26, 49, 50, 51, 52,
    119–20
  birdie or bogey and, 176
  fast swing and, 220, 222
Metropolitan Junior, 27
Middlecoff, Cary, 18
Mize, Larry, 184
Moroccan Open, 30

N

Nelson, Byron, 18
nervousness, 162
Newport Country Club, 146
Nicklaus, Jack "Golden Bear," 51, 58, 68,
    69, 70–71, 119, 127, 211
  Greg Norman and, 184, 185
9-iron, 65
Norman, Greg "Great White Shark," 12,
    39, 51, 71, 80, *81,* 85, *100,* 127,
    155, 157, 183, 207
  backswing and, 73–74, 99–100
  course management and, 120–22
  early career of, 184–86
  favorite club and, 125–26
  Fuzzy Zoeller and, 184, 185
  improved game of, 37–39, 76, *76,*
    119–20, 186
  interlocking grip of, 58, *58*
  Jack Nicklaus and, 184, 185
  new setup position of, 186–88, *188,*
    201–5
  new swing and, 190–92, *191*
  old setup position of, 186, *187,*
    200–201
  old swing of, 185, 189–90, *189*

square the clubface and, 83
tree-lined fairway and, 162

W

waggle, preswing, 68–70
Wall, Art, Jr., 57
water shot, 167–68
Watson, Tom, 51, 211
weak pop-ups with irons, 230
weak shots, reverse-pivots and, 179
wedges, 92–93, 168, 197
wedge shots:
    contact with ball on, 196–98, *197*
    Greg Norman and, 193–95
weight distribution:
    balance, backswing and, 73–75, 147
    stance and, 63–64, *64*, 66, 99
    topped shots with irons and, 227

wind conditions, 122–23, 164, 165, 176
Winged Foot Golf Club, 12, 19, 21, 23, 27, 86, 145, 150, 151, 153, 154, 156, 185
Wood, Craig, 19, 23, 151, 152, *152*
wood clubs:
    duck hook and, 233–35, *234*
    topped shots and, 224–26, *228*
Woods, Earl, 39
Woods, Tiger, 12, 39–41, 71, 119–20, 122–23, 210–16, *213*, *214*, *215*
wrist movement, 91

Y

yips, 101–2, 108

Z

Zoeller, Fuzzy, 184, 185

About the Authors

Claude Harmon, Jr., is currently the Director of Golf at Lochinvar Golf Club in Houston, Texas, where he teaches members how to play golf. Harmon is best known, however, for instructing PGA Tour pros Greg Norman and Davis Love III, and 1994 and 1995 United States Amateur champion Tiger Woods.

Harmon, who has taught the Shah of Iran and King Hassan II of Morocco, conducts regular trick shot exhibitions at tournaments and charity events and for major corporations.

Harmon is the son of Claude Harmon, Sr., one of golf's all-time best teachers and short-game players, who won the 1948 Masters.

John Andrisani is the senior editor of instruction at *GOLF Magazine*. He is also the coauthor of several books, including *Natural Golf* with Seve Ballesteros, *101 Supershots* with Chi Chi Rodriguez, *Grip It and Rip It!* with John Daly, and *The Golf Doctor* with Robin McMillan.

A fine player in his own right, Andrisani is a former course record holder, and a former winner of the American Golf Writers' Championship.

Leonard Kamsler is a New York–based photographer whose work appears regularly in *GOLF Magazine*.

Ken Lewis is a British artist who is recognized as one of the leading illustrators of the golf swing.